*And the Battle Began Like Claps of Thunder*

**Chester Harding, Daniel Boone. 1820**

# And the Battle Began like Claps of Thunder

## The Siege of Boonesborough – 1778

### As Told by the Pioneers

Compiled and Edited by

**Anne Crabb**

Heritage Books
2025

# HERITAGE BOOKS
*AN IMPRINT OF HERITAGE BOOKS, INC.*

**Books, CDs, and more—Worldwide**

For our listing of thousands of titles see our website
at
www.HeritageBooks.com

Published 2025 by
HERITAGE BOOKS, INC.
Publishing Division
5810 Ruatan Street
Berwyn Heights, MD 20740

Copyright © 1998, 2010 (revised edition)
Anne Crabb

Heritage Books by the author:

*And the Battle Began like Claps of Thunder;
The Siege of Boonesborough - 1778
As Told by the Pioneers*

*Warrior-Pioneers: Extracts from the Boone Papers,
Volumes 4C-13C of the Draper Manuscripts*

*Cover illustration is from the postcard
collection of Harry Johnson.*

All rights reserved. No part of this book may be reproduced or transmitted in any form or by any means, electronic or mechanical, including photocopying, recording or by any information storage and retrieval system without written permission from the author, except for the inclusion of brief quotations in a review.

International Standard Book Number
Paperbound: 978-0-7884-4843-0

*To the memory of all those who fought
in the siege of Boonesborough*

*To the memory of my father,
who told Daniel Boone stories*

*To those, past and present, who enrich our lives
through the tradition of oral history*

It was the year of 1778 that decision at Boonesborough came in an enormously exciting chain of events: the incidents at Blue Licks, the capture of the saltmakers, the escapes, the siege. September 16 was a cardinal date in the western revolutionary struggle. No historian is privileged to deal in terms of "if" but surely the survival of Boonesborough insured the survival of the remaining Kentucky settlements, and was a significant check on Indian-British attacks on the revolutionary frontier.

Thomas D. Clark

Dear Sir                                october the 5th 1809

The Later I Rec'd from you Respeting Squire Boones Surtevate Was Long Coming to hand and my Not being able to go to St Lewis I Dunn the Bisness before Col Reebby and Sent it on by Lewis Bryan in Closd in a Later to your Self and one to Squire Boone Directing him to Delever it to you him Self these Laters Could Not Reck you before you Left home if that Willnot Dow pleas Wright to me at St Charles and I will Make out another and Send it to you before Courte adjornes as I have the form you Sent me I am well in hailth But Deep in Morkury and Not able to Come Down I Shall Say Nothing about our petistion but Leve it all to your Self I am Dear is youres

Judge Colvren                           Daniel Boone

# Contents

| | |
|---|---|
| List of Illustrations | xi |
| Acknowledgments | xiii |
| Introduction | xv |
| Chronology | xvii |
| Prologue | xix |
| The Principal Narrators | xxiii |
| I. Before we start to Boonesborough | 1 |
| II. One man's life is worth 100 horses | 7 |
| III. How-dy Blackfish | 11 |
| IV. To live like Brothers | 15 |
| V. Flash after flash | 27 |
| VI. I ish a potter! | 31 |
| VII. Pour it to them, Billy, the day is a-rolling | 37 |
| VIII. Blow them all to h--l | 39 |
| IX. Providentially, the rain fell | 43 |
| Epilogue | 47 |
| Appendix | |
| Sources | 53 |
| Names of those in the Fort at Boonesborough during the siege | 59 |
| Boonesborough residents not present during the siege | 65 |
| Families at Fort Boonesborough during the siege | 66 |
| List of men of fighting age who may have participated in the siege | 69 |
| French and Indians at the siege | 70 |
| Miscellaneous biographical data | 71 |
| Petitions from Kentucky 1770's - 1780 | 101 |
| Militia men at Fort Boonesborough 1777-1778 | 103 |
| Companies of: | |
| Charles Gwatkins/Watkins | 103 |
| Richard May | 104 |
| Capt. Riddle | 104 |
| Kentucky Military Pensioners 1818-1840 | 104 |
| Lyman Draper's list of sources for the siege | 104 |
| Index | 107 |

was Entirely well when the Girls were taken or not he was well [crossed out] anuff to go along with the men that that pursued the Indians that Took the girls. he settled and was living on the north side of the Kentucky River at that time; left Kentucky with my father and joined a company of men to go on some Campaegn and in Mocenson gap the Indians fired on them and killed Mr Miller and he has no Decendants that I can Refer you to. Coper nor the Dutchman I know nothing off; nor Slaughter I know nothing off. You want to know whether at the time of the big Siege at Boonsborough there were any trees standing at the Indian Encampment or in the Flat grounds bounding along the little spring: answer there were a few Sycamore trees standing along the Branch near down to the spring and Plenty on the hills on Ellivated Ground joining the Frosty Ground, there was plenty of trees above the fort. having now Answered your Enquirie as well as my Recollection serves me I shall conclude by subscribing my self your sincere frund and hoping that you will get through in time and I will live to get a copy &c &c

John Gass

Lyman C Draper

**Letter from John Gass to Lyman Draper, November 6, 1848.** DM 24C 91(1)

# Illustrations

| | |
|---|---|
| Daniel Boone | Frontispiece |
| Daniel Boone Letter | viii |
| John Gass Letter | x |
| Map of Kentucky by Elihu Barker | xiv |
| Meeting of the Transylvania House of Delegates | xvi |
| Fort Boonesborough, September 1778 | xx |
| Fort Boonesborough and Surroundings | xxi |
| John Gass Photograph | xxii |
| Daniel Bryan Photograph | xxii |
| Moses Boone's Plat of Fort Boonesborough | xxiv |
| Map of the Early West | xxv |
| Arthur Campbell's Letter | 14 |
| Squire Boone Portrait | 22 |
| Flanders Callaway Sketch | 30 |
| Keziah Callaway Photograph | 38 |
| Climax of the Treaty | 44 |
| John Bowman Letter | 46 |
| Signatures of Pioneers | 52 |
| Black Hoof Portrait | 70 |
| Surveyor's Plat: Madison County, Kentucky | 106 |

## *Acknowledgments*

Much of the preparation for this book was done at Eastern Kentucky University Library's Special Collections and Archives where I had access to a complete set of the Draper Manuscripts, and sometimes, a good microfilm copier. Much additional information on the Boonesborough pioneers was found in this fine collection, although library visits resulted in numerous ten-dollar parking tickets.

I am especially indebted to Jerry Parrish Dimitrov, then Curator of the Townsend Collection of that library, for assistance in transcribing Draper manuscripts, suggesting further research possibilities, for reading the manuscript, and for help with illustrations. It was she who drew the composite plat of Fort Boonesborough, and who said "You might find something in the Draper Manuscripts." This book is the result of those findings. I thank Jacqueline Couture, library assistant of Special Collections and Archives, for helpful suggestions, especially with the keyed lists and computer problems, also for formatting and indexing the book. Rene Combs, library assistant at the time that I began working in the Draper Manuscripts, also helped with this project.

Ron Bryant, of the Kentucky Historical Society, read the manuscript and made time for consultations. I appreciate his insight and encouragement. Todd Moberly also read the manuscript and I appreciate his careful and colorful comments.

I am grateful to the following persons who supplied family records and/or court records: Kathleen Noland Calder, Jacqueline Couture, Diana C. Frymyer, and E. E. Puckett.

To those librarians of various county and university libraries who were able and eager to assist their patrons with unfailing courtesy, I say thank you.

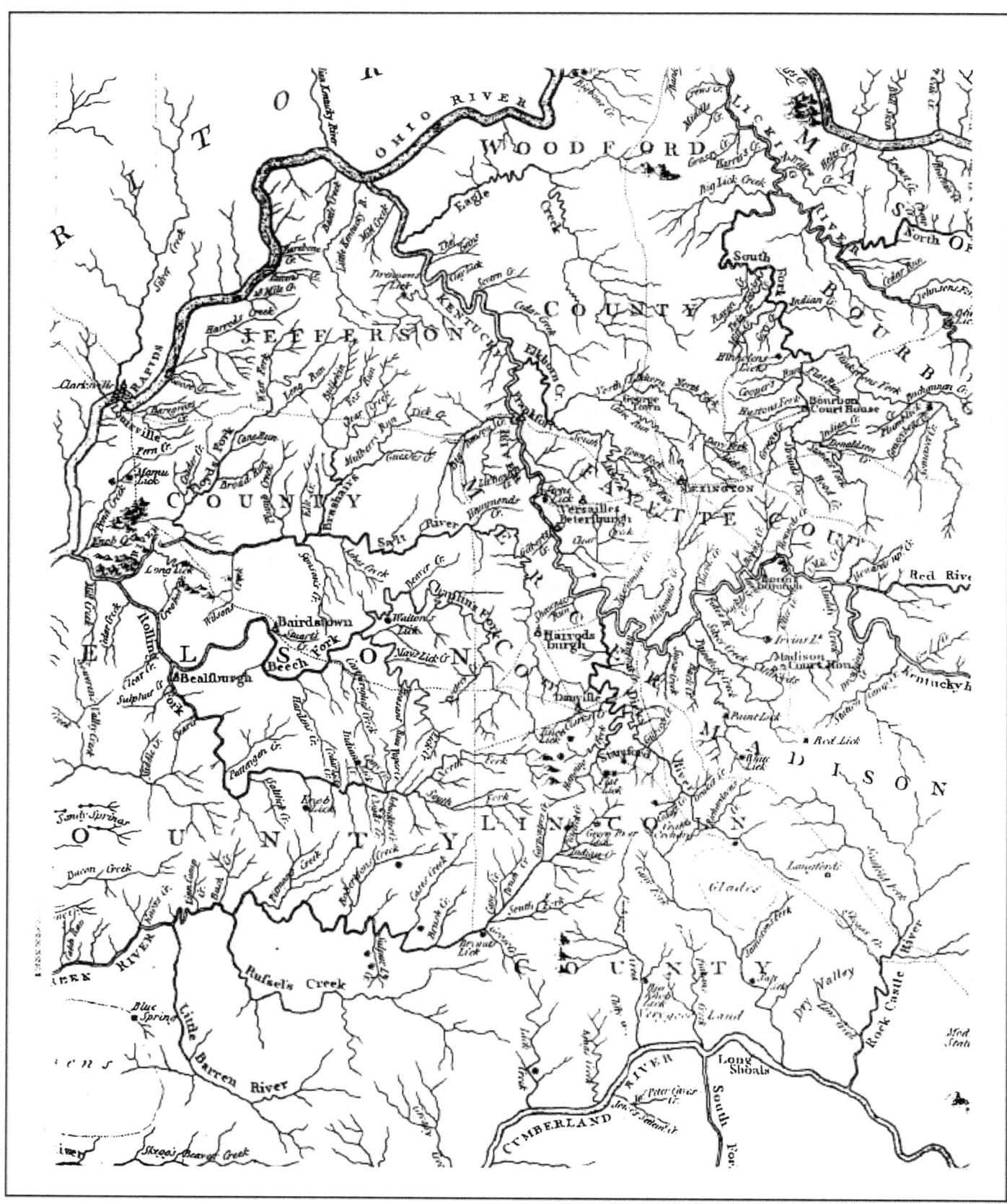

"Map of the State of Kentucky from Actual Survey by Elihu Barker of Philadelphia."
Printed in the Kentucky Historical Society Register, 21: 322-3 (Dec., 1923).

# Introduction

"The people in Boonesborough lived in friendship and harmony...they were as a large family," said pioneer Nicholas Proctor. Adversity, no stranger on the frontier, was a unifying force among people facing alarms and hardships daily. A hunter not returning with his party, Indian attacks, winters with no bread because it had been too dangerous to harvest the corn, a difficult birth or illness, the shortage of supplies such as salt needed to cure meat brought in by the hunters - such were their constant concerns. Yet they were a cheerful people. Weddings were celebrated with hilarity and watermelon feasts; tricks were played on novice hunters by veteran woodsmen pretending to be Indians. A typical meal might consist of a "sandwich" of bear meat between slabs of turkey meat instead of bread. On Sunday, the men put aside deerskin leggings in favor of the more cumbersome pantaloons to keep the Sabbath even in the Wilderness.

In the major event at Boonesborough, and one of the major events of Kentucky history, the sixty-odd residents of the fort and a few helpers from other forts made an astonishing effort of defense against about four hundred Indians and Frenchmen during the nine-days siege of Boonesborough in 1778. Not a major battle on the scale of Saratoga or Yorktown, the victory at Boonesborough nevertheless secured the western frontier (the Kentucky settlements) for the time being. The true losers in this event were the Indians, as the whites from both sides exploited their homelands and hunting grounds.

The thoughts and writings of Kentucky's famous and not-so-famous pioneers, such as John Gass and members of the Boone and Callaway families, are compiled here to tell the story of the siege of Boonesborough. Their telling, especially their eyewitness accounts, brings immediacy to an event which occurred over two hundred years ago.

Several of the pioneers, including some who were present, gave full accounts of the siege, while others supplied only a few facts (or contradictions). These accounts are excerpted and arranged chronologically, starting with Daniel Boone's escape from Indian captivity and return to Boonesborough in the summer of 1778. British and American military correspondence, contemporary letters and documents, and court records are interspersed to tell of the pioneers' and Indians' attempts to hold onto land which each perceived to be their own.

Most of the pioneer accounts were taken from the Draper Manuscripts which are held by the State Historical Society of Wisconsin. Drawn from an oral tradition tapped by two historians, Lyman Copeland Draper and the Rev. John Dabney Shane, these accounts provide a richness of detail found in no other source. The two tireless interviewers started in the 1840s by visiting the surviving pioneers, getting the stories in their own words or in letters (with their own spelling). The notebooks used to take down interviews were microfilmed "as is", with ink blots, notes in the margin, and faded ink; some words or whole pages are illegible.

Certain events were told again and again in much the same way, but contradictions occur as frequently as with today's witnesses of a particular event. Personalities emerge which would be recognizable in any community today.

In transcribing from Draper's and Shane's handwritten notes, the editor has spelled out abbreviations and added minimal punctuation and capitalization. Spelling is left as in the original. Pioneer usage includes "&c" which is equivalent to today's "etc". This is left intact in the letters quoted, as is "Colo" for Colonel. Daniel Boone, a captain at the time of the siege, was referred to as "Colo Boone", his later rank, by those telling the story. In pioneer usage, Indian battles took place between "whites" and "Indians" as a practical means of distinguishing between those engaged in the fighting. Question marks are inserted where illegible copy prevented certain transcribing. Comments within parentheses are those of Lyman Draper. Comments within brackets are those of the editor.

Meeting of the Transylvania House of Delegates, May, 1775
Designed from Historical Data by George W. Ranck

# Chronology of Events Effecting Fort Boonesborough

1750s-1774 - Kentucky, chiefly a hunting ground for Indian tribes, is explored by white men.

1774 in late spring - James Harrod builds the first cabin where Harrodsburg now stands

October 10, 1774 - The Shawnee Indians under Chief Cornstalk are defeated at the Battle of Point Pleasant.

December 1774 to February 1775 - Richard Henderson advertises land in Kentucky, solicits settlers to move there.

March 10?, 1775 - Daniel Boone and 30 woodcutters leave Virginia to cut the Wilderness Road

March 17, 1775 - Richard Henderson and the Cherokee Indians sign the Treaty of Watauga at Shoals.

March 20, 1775 - Henderson's Company leaves Virginia.

April 1, 1775 - Daniel Boone and his woodsmen arrive at what would become Boonesborough on the Kentucky River, having suffered an Indian attack with two fatalities at Twitty's Fort en route.

April 20, 1775 - Richard Henderson and his company of 40 men arrive about three weeks after Boone. Cabins built.

June 13, 1775 - Daniel Boone and Richard Callaway return to Virginia to bring their families back to Kentucky.

Sept. 8, 1775 - Daniel Boone returns to Boonesborough with his family and about 25 settlers.

Late September 1775 - Richard Callaway returns to Boonesborough with his family, William Pogue's family and Barney Stagner's family.

March, 1776 - St. Asaph's or Logan's Fort settled by Benjamin Logan with his wife and children.

July 14?, 1776 - Daniel Boone's daughter Jemima and two of Richard Callaway's daughters, Betsy and Fanny, are captured from Boonesborough by Indians and recovered 3 days later.

Summer 1776 - Two Boonesborough weddings: Betsy Callaway and Samuel Henderson; Jemima Boone and Flanders Callaway.

December 6, 1776 - The Virginia Assembly creates Kentucky County from Fincastle County, Virginia. Kentucky is now a part of Virginia, "one distinct county".

March 1777 - Lord George Germain orders British commanders in America to arm the Indians and set them against the western settlements.

March, April, May 1777 - Indians attack Fort Boonesborough three times, other Kentucky forts sustain attacks.

July 25, 1777 - A company of 45 men arrive from North Carolina.

August or September, 1777 - Colonel Bowman with Captains Pawling and Dunkin arrive in Kentucky with 100 Virginia militia.

September 13, 1777 - Capt. William Bailey Smith's Company of about 48 men arrives (John Holder, Lieutenant) from the North Carolina Yadkin country.

October 13[?] 1777 - Capt. Charles G. Watkins (called Gwatkins by George Rogers Clark) arrives with a company of 50 men from Bedford County, Virginia.

October 1777 - Cornstalk, Shawnee Chief, is killed by Virginia soldiers at Point Pleasant in western Virginia. Burgoyne is defeated at Saratoga, ending Britain's plan to win the war in 1777, and leading the French to enter the war on the side of the Americans.

January 2, 1778 - George Rogers Clark receives orders from Gov. Patrick Henry to plan a secret attack on British posts. Some of his men are to gather at Boonesborough.

January 7 or 8 - Salt-making expedition begins. Daniel Boone and 28[?] men leave the fort at Boonesborough for Lower Blue Licks. Only a few older or wounded men are left to guard the fort.

February 7 - Indians capture Daniel Boone.

February 8 - Indians capture the salt makers at their camp.

March 26 - Captains Dillard and Donelson arrive with 80 men at Boonesborough. Daniel Trabue and Josiah Collins arrive at this time.

May - Mrs. Daniel Boone and her younger children, thinking Daniel dead, return to the Yadkin settlement escorted by her son-in-law, William Hays.

May - Daniel Boone observes preparations for the intended attack on Boonesborough during his captivity.
June - William Bailey Smith's expedition across the Ohio
June 14 - Henry Hamilton reports to Frederick Haldimand that a council is held at Detroit of more than 1600 Indians representing many tribes, with several Frenchmen, gifts given the Indians, etc.
June 16 - Daniel Boone escapes from the Indians.
June 20 - Daniel Boone arrives at Boonesborough.
June 24 - George Rogers Clark and 153 men leave Falls of the Ohio [Louisville] for Kaskaskia.
July 4 - George Rogers Clark takes Kaskaskia.
July 17 - William Hancock reaches Boonesborough after escaping from the Indians three weeks earlier. An express [messenger] is sent to Virginia asking for help for the expected siege against Boonesborough.
August - British and Americans prepare for siege
August 31 - Daniel Boone leads about 30 men on the Paint Creek Expedition to spy on the Indians.
September 7 - Boone and all but four? men return, passing the Indian army at Blue Licks
September 8 - Two late-returning men of the Paint Creek Expedition arrive at Boonesborough in the morning. Indians under Black Fish and some Frenchmen arrive at Boonesborough, ask Boone to surrender. People in the fort decide not to surrender, and to stall for time in hope of help arriving from Virginia.
September 9 - Boone and Black Fish agree to hold treaty talks.
September 10 - Treaty talks held. Fighting breaks out.
September ?? - William Stafford returns from a hunting trip, observes the siege in progress, reports to Logan's Station that Boonesborough has fallen.
September 18 or 19? - Indians depart. Indians seen around Logan's Station.
September? - Daniel Boone is court-martialled at Logan's Station, receives promotion to Major, returns to North Carolina to bring his family back to Kentucky.
October 1778 - The Virginia Assembly grants Richard Henderson a tract of land in western Kentucky, declaring that while the purchase from Cherokee Indians is void, the Commonwealth is likely to receive benefit from Henderson's efforts toward increasing its inhabitants.
1779 - Daniel Boone and family settle at Boone's Station in Fayette County, no longer live at Boonesborough.
February 1779 - George Rogers Clark takes Vincennes, captures Henry Hamilton, who is taken through Kentucky to Charlottesville where he is imprisoned.
Summer 1779 - Black Fish, Shawnee chief, is killed by white men during Bowman's Campaign.
March 1780 - Richard Callaway and Pemberton Rollins are killed by Indians while supervising the building of a ferry boat.
March 10, 1780 - Petition from the inhabitants of Boonesborough to George Rogers Clark asking for a campaign against the Indian towns in Ohio to put the Indians on the defensive and save Kentucky's forts.

# *Prologue*

On the eve of battle in western Virginia in 1774, Shawnee Chief Cornstalk instructed his warriors at the council held before the Battle of Point Pleasant:

See you that towering oak! Thus are the whites now grown strong, and we cannot uproot... we had better make peace.

I am no coward - if my nation resolves to continue the war, I will lead my warriors to the battlefield, and then it shall be seen who are the cowards.

The Shawnee warriors did not seek peace with the white intruders. During the battle which followed, Cornstalk was observed by a former prisoner of the Shawnee. Riding a fine white horse up and down the Indian line, he exhorted his warriors:

Be strong! be strong! - be men! be men!

Afterward, in their Indian village, Cornstalk told his people:

"What," said he, "will you do now? The Big Knife is coming on us, and we shall all be killed. Now you must fight, or we are undone." But no one made an answer. He said, "then let us kill all our women and children, and go and fight until we die". But none would answer. At length he rose and struck his tomahawk in the post in the centre of the town house: "I'll go," said he, "and make peace..."

Within months of Cornstalk's prophesy, the Cherokee Indians sold what they probably perceived to be hunting or grazing rights in Kentucky to a group of white men. The purchasers, headed by Richard Henderson, called themselves the Transylvania Company. Henderson had already sent Daniel Boone and a party of men to open the Wilderness Road and establish Fort Boonesborough; Henderson expected to profit from land sales (of questionable legality from the start) by enticing settlers to Kentucky. But Kentucky was the hunting ground not only of the Cherokees, as Kentucky pioneer Chilton Allen stated:

...Kentucky was in the midst of an interminable wilderness. Five thousand Indians regarded it as their hunting ground.

For the first few months after the treaty-signing in western Virginia only small groups of white men lived in Kentucky, mostly at Boonesborough, Harrodsburg, and Logan's Fort. They selected land, planted corn, built cabins, hunted. That fall, several of the Kentucky hunters returned to Virginia and North Carolina to bring their families out. This alarmed the Indians very much, as their hunting ground was threatened if settlements were established in Kentucky.

**Fort Boonesborough, September, 1778**
**Designed from Historical Data by George W. Ranck**

To those building cabins and planting corn in Kentucky, the land was theirs by treaty or by "making an improvement" upon it. Under land laws of the late 1770's, settlers could get four hundred acres for making "improvements", that is building cabins and planting corn on Kentucky land. Little was known about the Indian way of life except by those who had lived among the Indians after being captured. (A significant proportion of those captives chose to remain among the Indians when offered their freedom.) To the average settler, however, ownership of land south of the Kentucky River had been fairly sanctioned in the treaty with the Cherokees. They knew little and cared less that various Indian tribes claimed Kentucky for their hunting ground. All Indians were "savages". To the Indians, the white settlers were a threat to centuries of Indian life. Indian leaders began to see that the new white settlements would not only deprive them of their hunting ground, but would slowly push them off their homeland.

The Indians began isolated attacks on Kentucky's forts about 1776; the raids continued in sporadic fashion until 1778. These attacks were perpetrated mostly by smaller war parties, usually of the Shawnee or Wyandot tribes. There were some sustained attacks on the forts at Harrodsburg, Boonesborough, and Logan's.

In the fall of 1777, Cornstalk went to make peace with the Virginians and was killed by white soldiers while on this peaceful mission. The murder of Cornstalk provoked a revenge of huge proportions upon white settlers on the frontier, an effort encouraged by the British. Instead of sending small war parties, Indian tribes now united in an effort to rid the frontier of the unwanted settlements. With British backing, and armed by their British sponsors, a combined war party of about four hundred was sent to Kentucky in 1778. On this expedition, however, they did not bring cannon, or "swivels", as they were called.

Cannon had not yet been seen in Kentucky, except for one built by Squire Boone at Boonesborough. Daniel Boone had attempted to bring a cannon over the Wilderness Road but was unsuccessful, the trail not being wide enough. In 1778, a messenger arriving at Boonesborough brought news that a cannon was being brought for the expected attack, so those in the fort were expecting to face cannon fire.

Perhaps the Indian way of thinking was: if Boonesborough fell, all Kentucky forts would fall; all the intruders would return to the settlements eastward or be taken prisoner and converted to the British cause, bringing so much bounty per head. The settlement of Kentucky by white people would be ended.

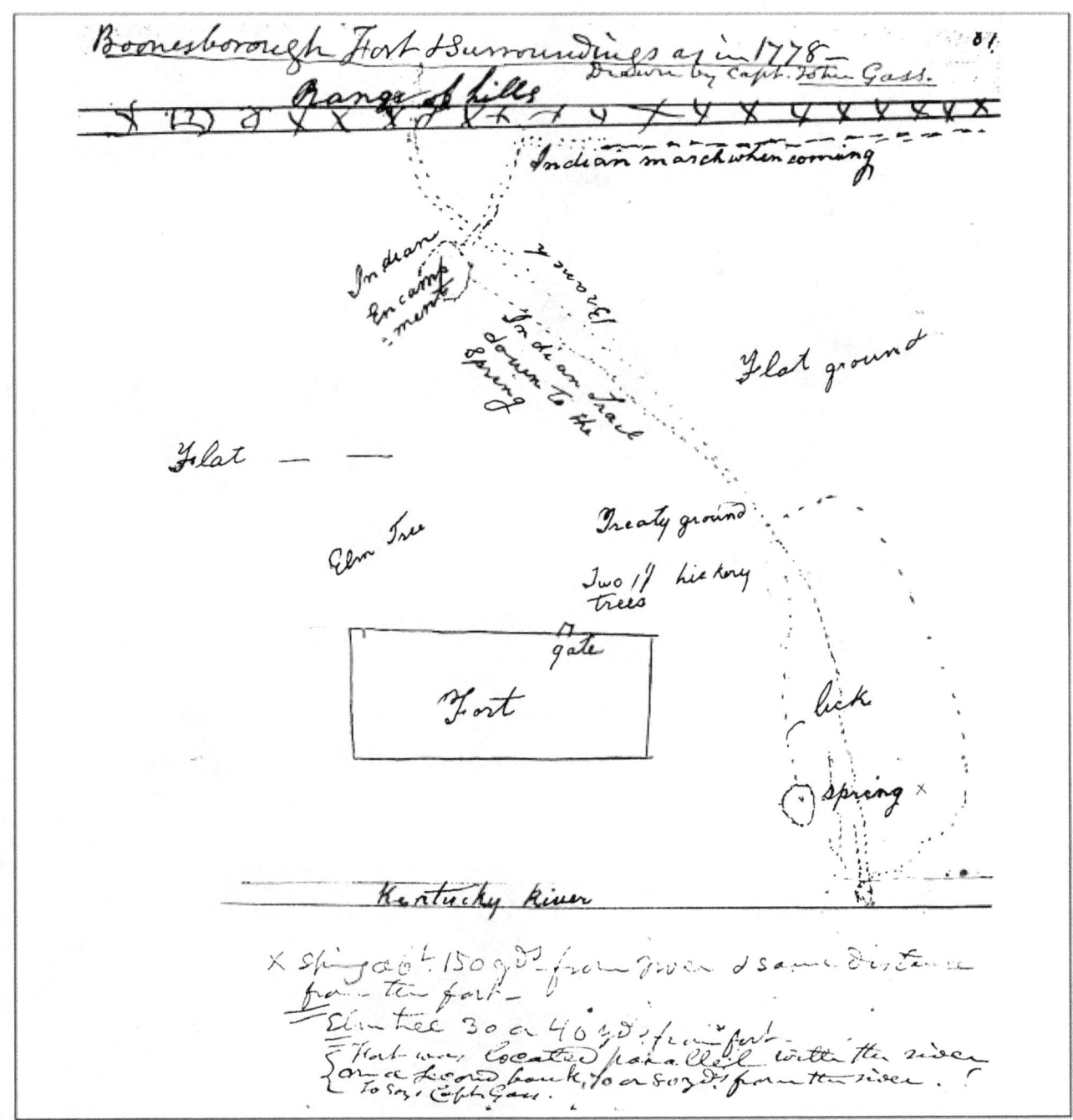

**Fort Boonesborough and Surroundings**
**Drawn by John Glass in a letter to Lyman Draper in 1848. DM 24C 89**

**John Gass.** Courtesy of the State Historical Society of Wisconsin

**Daniel Bryan.** Courtesy of the State Historical Society of Wisconsin

## *The Principal Narrators*

The accounts of many relatives and contemporaries of the Kentucky pioneers are compiled here to tell the story of the siege. A few of these persons supplied plentiful and vivid information. Since their accounts appear frequently, drawn from their letters and interviews, they are introduced here.

**Narrators living at Boonesborough who were eyewitnesses to the siege:**

Moses Boone, age 9, son of Squire Boone

Isaiah Boone, age 6, son of Squire Boone

John Gass, age 14, son of David Gass

**Accounts by contemporaries living near Boonesborough at the time of the siege:**

Daniel Trabue, a young man living at Logan's Fort

Daniel Bryan, Mrs. Daniel (Rebecca) Boone's cousin

Josiah Collins, arrived at Boonesborough in March, 1778

**Accounts of descendants of Daniel and Rebecca Boone:**

Nathan Boone, born 1781, youngest son of Daniel Boone

Delinda Boone Craig, daughter of Nathan

Susan Howell, daughter of Jemima Boone Callaway and Flanders Callaway

Serena Howell, grand-daughter of Jemima and Flanders

Evisa L. Coshow, grand-daughter of Jemima and Flanders

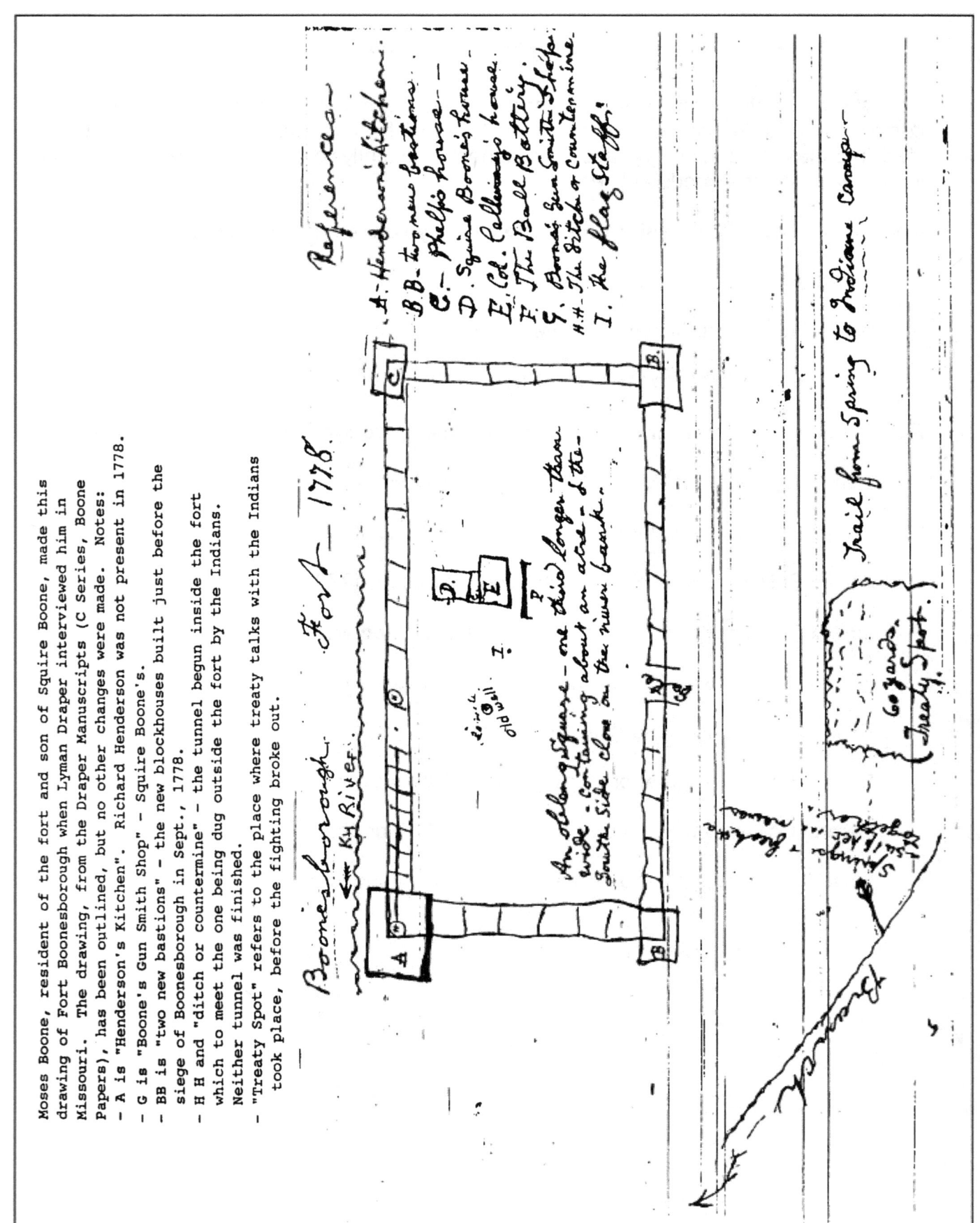

Moses Boone's Plat of Fort Boonesborough in 1778 drawn during an interview with Lyman Draper.

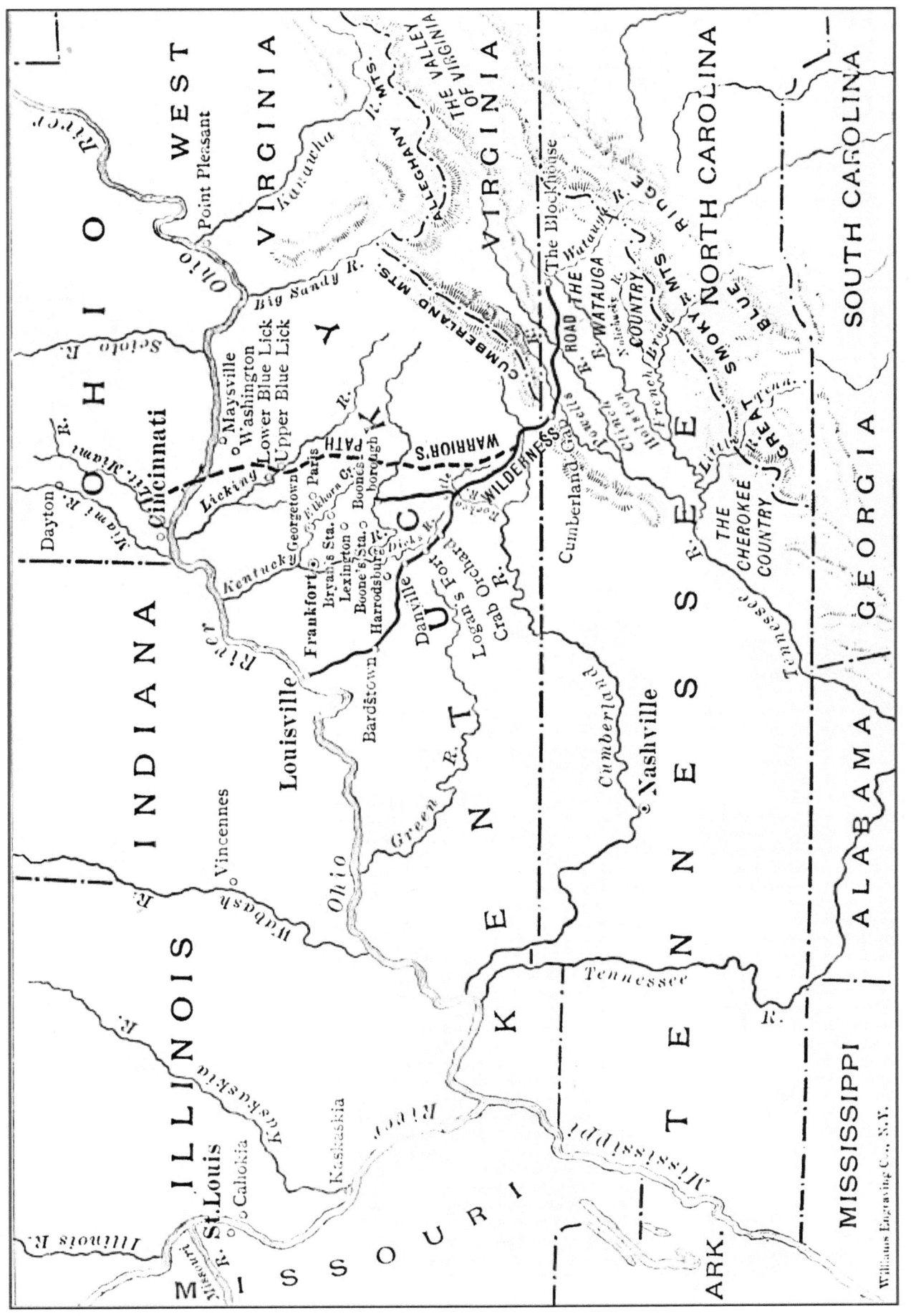

Map of the Early West from Daniel Boone and the Wilderness Road, H. Addington, New York: The Macmillian Co., 1910

# *Chapter I.*

## *Before we start to Boonesborough*

Moving silently southward through the wilderness, rafting the Ohio River on saplings tied together with grapevine, Daniel Boone covered the distance from the Chillicothe Indian village to Boonesborough in four days. He had lived among the Shawnee as a captive and adopted son of Chief Blackfish for four months, and had overheard plans for a late summer or fall attack on Fort Boonesborough. This would not have surprised him, for he had promised to surrender the fort and its inhabitants, including his own family, when he was captured in February, 1778. He had promised that the surrender would take place the following summer.

Daniel Boone had no intention of honoring his duplicitous promise to Black Fish, a promise made when he found a large party of Indians planning to attack Fort Boonesborough in wintertime when it would have been poorly defended. The Indians had found him while he was out hunting in the snow near the camp of a company of salt makers from Boonesborough. Boone then diverted the Indians to this camp at Blue Licks where about twenty-six prisoners could be taken without firing a shot. Hoping to distract the Indians from their original plan of making prisoner those in the fort, Boone explained that traveling in winter would be too hard on the women and children, no doubt fearing for his own wife and children. The Indians showed him horses they had brought for them to ride, and Boone convinced them to bring the horses back in the summer and he would surrender the inhabitants of the fort then.

Boone and his men, those who survived, spent the next months or years in captivity; only a few escaped during the first six months after capture. Two of the escapees undertook the risky journey from Ohio to Kentucky in the summer of 1778: Daniel Boone and William Hancock, both Indian adoptees, had observed elaborate preparations in their Indian towns for the expected surrender of Boonesborough to the Indians. They had to warn the fort of the hundreds of warriors who would soon appear before its walls expecting Boone to honor his promise. Boone arrived at Boonesborough on June 20, 1778. Hancock arrived a few weeks later.

The events of 1778 were described years later in Missouri where Daniel Boone received a visitor who apparently knew him during his captivity. Conversations between two former adversaries, Daniel Boone and Indian Phillips, were overheard by Daniel's grandson, John C. Boone. The story, told in first person as if John C. Boone were Indian Phillips, presents the Indian viewpoint of events preceding the siege of Boonesborough. The terms under which Boone agreed to surrender the fort, the preparations for the attack on Boonesborough, and Boone's escape are described:

> ...Dan, when we had you prisoner at Detroit, you rember the British traders gave you a horse, Saddle & bridle...our Chief [Black Fish] adopted you as his Son & you & he made an agreement that you would all go to Boonsboro, and you would

make them all surrender and all bury the Tomahack & all live like brothers and Sisters.

Then you rember we were all glad & Black Fish said to you one pretty warm day, Dan the corn is in good roasting ears, and I would like to have your horse and mine in good order before we start to Boonsborough, but we have no trough to feed them in, so get the Ax[?] and go with me and I will show you a big log that you can dig out. So you went and he poot [put] you to work a big walnut log, and you worked a while, got tired and lay down.

By and by Black Fish come along, and Said, well Dan you haven't done much, you answered and Said, No you and your Squaw calles me your Son, and this dont look like you love me, when I am at home I don't do this kind of work...

Then you rember we started for Boons Borough and a few miles before we reached the Sciota Salt lick we all scattered out to kill some game, and let you go with the Squaws and you had some brass kittles tied together with raw hide strings swinging across your Saddle, and when you arrived at the Salt Lick, the Squaws all dismounted, but you Set on your horse and took your knife and cut the strings and let the kittles fall to the ground, then your Indian Mother said what are you going to do Dan, and you answered, I am going to see my wife and children, and your mother said you had better not, if you go Black Fish will be mad, and you said I don't care if he is, I am going to see my wife and children, and imediatly the Squaw began to whoop for the Warriors[?] and you put whip to your Horse and when we came, we took your horses tracks and pursued nearly all day till we came to a creek that was Swolen[?] from bank to bank there we found your horse gave out...a vine the top of which was fast to the top of a tree on the oposite side, with which you swang yourself across...

Here we held a council, and they all said let you go, that you would never git home, you would Starve to death, but I told them that you would get home for you went as straight as a leather string.

Then as it was our custom when a prisoner escaped, we made no move for 10 days. That delay gave you time to git home - Take a pirogue of men and go back and destroy our corn &c and back to your fort before we reached there.

After Daniel Boone reached Boonesborough, he began repairs to the fort. An express [messenger] was sent to Virginia asking for help for the impending attack. Daniel found his family had returned to North Carolina during his long absence. The only members of his family who were present at his return were his brother Squire and family, and his married daughter, Jemima Callaway. Daniel's daughter-in-law, Mrs. Nathan Boone [Olive VanBibber], later told of his disappointment when he found his family gone:

[Boone] was much disappointed to learn his family had gone to Carolina. Went[?] to his old house - & found his family cat had deserted it from the time when Mrs.

Boone left - within half an hour after Col. Boone's return, came & fondled around & jumped into his lap.

A letter from John Todd to Patrick Lockhart of Botetourt County, Virginia and dated "Harrodsburg 29th June 1778" announced the news of Boone's arrival in Kentucky: "Capt. Boone has runaway from the Shawanese & arrived with abundance of News. &c &c. Indians appear frequently among us & generally of late unsuccessful..."

Todd gave the news that George Rogers Clark had taken sixty men from Harrodsburg [he also took men from Boonesborough] to strike Kaskaskia, which was defeated on July 4, 1778. These men, probably on a three-month enlistment, missed the siege of Boonesborough.

Several weeks after Daniel Boone and his salt makers were captured, Capt. Thomas Dillard and a company of men from Virginia arrived at Boonesborough on March 26, 1778. Conditions at the fort that spring were described Josiah Collins, a member of the company:

..found there a party of poor, desolate and distressed people, almost without provisions and with very little clothing and what added most to their distress was their exposure to constant alarm from the Indians who were very troublesome. They had meat to procure from the forest, always in danger of losing their lives.

The fort was still in a dismal state of repair months later while so many men were absent during their captivity. Two young boys then living in the fort were later interviewed by Lyman Draper and told of the preparations which were made after Daniel Boone's return. John Gass, then in his early teens, recalled:

...the fort was in a dilapidated state...built bastions, and finished stockading, and the old well not affording a sufficiency of water, commenced digging a new well but did not complete it. An express was sent to Colo Arthur Campbell for aid; and it was all important to gain time.

Squire Boone's son Moses, age nine at the time of the siege, later told Draper:

Corn [was] gathered and brought into the cabin lofts, and made his little expedition [the Paint Creek Expedition] as the Indians had not appeared so early as he expected. New stockading added, & the fort enlarged towards the east, new bastions added at the southeast & southwest corners, the 2nd story built up height of a man's head, omitting roof, no time.

Fort Boonesborough at first was simply several cabins built by Daniel Boone and about thirty men who cut the Wilderness Trail in 1775 as employees of Richard Henderson, whose men then followed Boone to Kentucky. The cabins they built were relocated to higher ground at Henderson's insistence. Richard Henderson's diagram of the fort shows eight cabins on the longer sides and five on each of the shorter sides for a total of twenty-six cabins.

As stated by various pioneers, bastions or blockhouses were completed in 1778 so the four corners projecting outward would contain what the pioneers called "portholes" to shoot through. These bastions, built in haste, were not roofed. Picketing was added to enclose the fort which had been partly open. The cabins had been roofed with inward-slanting wooden shingles; these were easily removed if set on fire. Picketing between cabins could be eased in places to allow entrance if the main gate was not safe. Such an entrance provided safety for some during the siege. The main entrance was a large gate on the side away from the river. There may have been one or two smaller gates; even those who lived at the fort disagree about the number of gates. The fort was described and drawn by Bland Ballard, who lived at Boonesborough with the Callaway family during the 1770's. [The Bland Ballard information is almost illegible; only a few words can be transcribed.]

> The fort was kept clean - also the barracks were kept clean...the fort was picketed between the cabins where they did not join...

> The side of the fort next to the river was f---tested[?] the whole length of heavy timber about 10 feet out of the ground & the houses on that side were within the pickets. The big gate was made ---- solid with heavy timber, with iron bars across & heavy iron hi--g---- [hingeing?]. The little gate was used for people to go down to the river of wash days...

    A blacksmith shop belonging to Squire Boone stood in the middle of the fort. The fort's flag flew atop a pole in the center area, on which was mounted a wooden gun (fashioned by Squire Boone) which served as a weathervane.
    Located outside the fort were two springs, one fresh water and one sulphur, and a tree known as the divine elm. Tree stumps which had not been removed when the land was cleared provided hiding places for the Indians when they had tried to approach the fort at various times.
    The fort, after the improvements of the summer of 1778, was probably as described by a young man, Michael Bedinger, who came to Boonesborough one year later:

> The fort was a parallelogram, about two hundred and fifty feet long, and one hundred twenty-five feet wide. At each corner was a two-storied block house; inside were well-built log-cabins, so constructed that their outer sides formed part of the wall. The entire enclosure was surrounded by high stockades, made of heavy timbers thrust upright into the ground, and bound together by a horizontal stringer. Each cabin was separately defensible, and in times of danger the horses and cattle were driven into the open square in the middle of the enclosure.

Daniel Trabue, of Logan's Fort, supplied the definition of "blockhouse":

> What is ment by a block house? The uper story to be much biger than the lower story and to Jut over so that you may be up on the uper floor and shot Down if the indeans was to come up to the walls, and they cannot climb up the walls of these houses.

    Josiah Collins had left Boonesborough a few weeks before the siege to live at Harrodsburg, but some of his company, Dillard's men, remained at Boonesborough and participated in the siege. Doubtless some of them were present when the second captive arrived at Boonesborough that summer with news of the expected attack. This man was one of Boone's surrendered salt makers, William Hancock.

Having heard the plans to attack Boonesborough from his adopted Indian father, Captain Will, Hancock realized the urgency of the situation and wanted to warn the fort, not knowing that Boone, held captive in another village, had already returned to give the news. Hancock escaped with great difficulty with no food or clothing. (The Indians, being suspicious that he might try to escape, confiscated his clothes at night.) In crossing the Ohio River, he was carried downstream too far, and soon was lost. It was three weeks before he reached the fort, almost naked and nearly starved. When he arrived at the Kentucky River, he was so weak that his cries were barely heard by those in the fort. A canoe was sent to bring him across the river. Hancock gave the warning of the impending attack, and blamed Boone for it, saying he sold out to the Indians by promising to surrender the fort.

Immediately after William Hancock returned to Boonesborough, letters were drafted and sent by express to Virginia asking for help. These urgent messages, called "the Kentucky Packet", contained letters (one from Boone) and William Hancock's deposition:

Boonesborough, 17th July, 1778

Kentucky SS
The deposition of William Hancock, being first sworn on the Holy Evangelists, is as follows: ...the Indians informed, they should come four hundred strong, and offer the English flag to the inhabitants, and if the terms were rejected, they intended to batter down our fort with their swivels [cannon], as they are to have four sent them from Detroit, which will be conveyed up the Mawmee river, and down the Great Miami to the Ohio, and thence up the Kentucky to Boonesborough.

This was the day that Hancock arrived at Boonesborough in such a weakened state after escaping from Indian captivity. The Indians were not able to get the expected cannon to Kentucky on this trip. Daniel Boone's letter to "Colonels Arthur Campbell or Evan Shelby" was written the following day. An excerpt follows:

Boonesborough, 18th July, 1778.

Dear Colonel:
...If men can be sent out to us in five or Six weeks, it would be of infinite service, as we shall lay up provisions for a siege. We are all in fine spirits, and have good crops growing, and intend to fight hard in order to secure them. I shall refer you to the bearer for particulars of this country.

I am yours &c
Daniel Boone

To Cols. Arthur Campbell,
or Evan Shelby

In less than two weeks, the Kentucky Packet was in the hands of Col. Arthur Campbell in western Virginia. His letter to the Governor and Council of Virginia at Williamsburg shows that some military support was being organized for the forts in Kentucky. Arthur Campbell expressed the difficulties of persuading officials to support the western frontier when they were fully occupied with the British in the East. A delay followed, as Campbell waited, or was forced to wait, before sending the requested aid to Kentucky.

> Washington [County, Virginia]
> July 3l 1778
>
> Sir:
> By the enclosed Copy of a Letter and deposition will be made known the probable distress of the Garrison at Boonesborough. ...by the accounts of the prisoners[?] the Commandant at Detroit [Henry Hamilton] has effectually set against us the most vindictive Indian Tribe Yet[?]. No doubt he profits much in a private way by the plunder of our frontier. I propose sending Major [Daniel]Smith of This County with some Militia to the relief of Kentucky... I think I can raise two [companies]... and I hope to have Them ready to March from the Neighborhood of Mockison Gap by the l5th day of August. Should not There be a call for Militia to go on the Expedition? I hope the relief of Kentucky may prove an essential[?] service. I have sent on the Kentucky packet to [Williamsburg] by Express as assind and expect an Answer will be back...by the l5th of next month. ...attention is too much enjoyed with the affairs Eastwardly or else They don't feel for the miseries that happen on the Western frontier.
>
> I am Sir Your very Humble....
> Arthur Campbell

The response from the Governor and Council of Virginia to the Kentucky Packet and Campbell's letter was made on August 12th. Col. Arthur Campbell was directed to send not less than one hundred militia "officered in the usual manner" to the relief of Kentucky.

British correspondence made the rounds advising of preparations for the expedition. In a letter written August 17, Henry Hamilton, Lieutenant Governor of Detroit, quoted one of the renegade Girty brothers (much respected among the Indians): "four hundred Indians have gone to attack 'Fort Kentuck'."

Mrs. Nathan Boone told of the delay in the expected siege, and how Boone used this time:

> A prisoner returned, [Hancock] reporting that in consequence of Boone's escape the Indian Expedition against Boonesboro had been postponed two weeks, & an express sent [by the Indians] to Gov. Hamilton notifying him of Boone's escape & the postponement - seemingly waiting further orders from him. Learning this postponement, the repairing of the fort was now delayed - & Boone carried on the Paint Creek Expedition.

## Chapter II.

## *One man's life is worth 100 horses*

The Paint Creek Expedition began at the end of August, 1778. The small company of men from Boonesborough and Logan's Fort just barely made it back before several hundred Indians appeared before the fort at Boonesborough asking for Daniel Boone. The adventures of this company of men were told by some of the participants and their descendants.

The reasons for the expedition probably had something to do with Daniel Boone's curiosity about what the Indians were up to and boredom with making repairs to the fort. For men accustomed to hunting and scouting, simply waiting for the Indians to arrive must have been unbearable. Daniel Boone and men from various Kentucky forts made up a company to do some Indian hunting and horse hunting. The Indians had stolen so many horses that year that William Whitley, who lived near Logan's Station, complained that they had to carry the meat from hunting expeditions to the fort on their backs. (Whitley had signed on for a horse-hunting expedition the previous spring.) So much horse stealing went on that the Indians and Kentuckians actually swapped the same horses back and forth.

The idea of horse-hunting was an enticement to the volunteer company and the possibility of taking Indian prisoners who could reveal enemy plans to the settlers was probably on Daniel Boone's mind. Creating a diversion might put the Indians on the defensive and avert the intended attack on Boonesborough.

This was the third such expedition from Boonesborough in 1778. In May, escaped captive Andrew Johnson, one of Boone's salt makers, led a group of Kentucky men across the Ohio River to spy on the Indians. In June, William Bailey Smith led a group of Boonesborough men across the river into a skirmish with the Indians. Daniel Boone heard of this incident while still captive, and doubtless would have participated in it had he been free.

Josiah Collins, an intelligent man with a remarkable memory, was interviewed by Rev. John D. Shane about the June expedition:

> A little before I left Boonesborough [Collins perhaps moved to Harrodsburg in summer of 1778], a party from that place went in pursuit of a party of Indians that had stolen horses and gone down towards the Ohio. They got in between two parties, as they (the whites) discovered by the fire of a gun. They then stopped, tied their horses behind them, with the moon behind them and formed a half moon, till the other party came up. The surprise would have been complete, but Ephraim Drake fired too soon, and the Indians having dismounted, fled. Boone afterwards asked Blackfish, who was one of them [with the Indians], why he didn't fight. He replied, clapping his hands very fast...(indicating too many shots fired).

Lyman Draper gave this account of the same expedition, indicating that Ephraim Drake fired at the Indian to save the horses retrieved from the Indians:

> Early in June, a party of Shawanoes stole several horses from Boonesborough, when Maj. William Bailey Smith, Capt. David Gass, John Martin, Ephraim Drake,

John Clark, and 13 others, mounted on horseback, started in pursuit; and reaching the Ohio at the present locality of Maysville, they found some Indians crossing the stream, and succeeded in killing one of their number. Returning in the evening along the old buffalo and Indian trace leading to the Lower Blue Licks they when 4 miles from the river, where the town of Washington now stands, they discovered by hearing a loud laugh, another Indian party encamped, consisting of about 30 warriors, who proved to be the very marauders of whom they were in search. Smith's men fell back, tied their horses, and while one half remained there as a guard with directions to rush forward if they heard an attack, Smith with the others crept along nearly to the Indian encampment, and placed themselves on either side of the buffalo road. At length one of the Indians, hearing a noise which he thought indicated the proximity of a fox, walked towards the whites leisurely smoking his pipe, armed only with a bow and arrows. He was suffered [allowed] to pass all the men except the last, Ephraim Drake, who knew if the Indian was permitted to advance any farther, he would discover the horses; when Drake shot him...the Indian uttering a dying yell... His companions at first raised a hearty laugh, thinking he had...killed the fox... In the ensuing skirmish, John Martin was wounded in the shoulder... He was taken to Boonesborough where his wound was dressed...by Jesse Hodges.

Daniel Trabue, who lived at Logan's Fort, was all set for the next expedition in August before his older brother talked him out of it. He described the reasons for the Paint Creek Expedition and preparations for it:

The endians stole almost all the horses we had belonging to Logan's Fort. Some men had been to the indean towns and stole horses and had good suckess in the adventer. Alexander Montgomery and Simon Kenton asked me if I would go with them to the Indian town to steal horses, and I and G. Clark agreed to go. We 4 agreed to go to Scioto wher Chillicothey now is. We made preparation to go, got some nise halters made with grained raw Buffelow hides. We procured Deer lether lagons [leggings], parched corn Meal, and some Jirk. With 2 pair Mockinsons to each man, etc., our guns and ammunition in the best Order, the next morning we was to start...

He [brother James] came to me and talked to me about this Matter. I told him that he knew the indeans had got my horse and we could go and steel horses from them. It was much better to Do that than to give my Mony for a horse... James Replyed, "It is a Dangerous attempt. I am not willing for you to hazard your life in that way. One man's life is worth 100 horses and you have got mony a plenty that you brought from home with you... A horse can be got when you want one to go home on...if any thing would happin to you how could I Ever see our Mother? She would say, 'James, how come you to lit Daniel go on such an errand?' I concluded I would not go...

But they would have time to go against Jest some indians that lived not far over the Ohio, and if a few men would go with him [Boone] he would conduct them to this little Camp, and as these indians was rich in good horses and beaver fur, they could go and make a great speck and Git back in good time to oppose the big army of Indians...

Another member of the company was Stephen Hancock, brother of William who had just escaped from the Indians:

...went with Colonel Boone, Colonel John Logan, John Kennedy and others amounting in all to about 28 men to see whether we could discover any Indians and we traveled said salt lick trace from Boonesborough and went to Lower Blue Licks...

Jesse Hodges, also a member of the company, stated in a deposition in 1817:

...in 1778 he started from Boonesborough, to take an Indian town on Paint Creek, in a company of 18 men, viz.: Daniel Boone, Simon Canton [Kenton], now called Simon Butler, John Cannady [Kennedy], John Logan, John Holder, Pemberton Rollins, John Callaway, Edmond Fear, Alex Montgomery, John Stapleton, and the others not recollected. ...We crossed the Ohio River near the mouth of Cabin Creek. Simon Canton was our best pilot; the company depended on him to show the way; he was a good woodsman.

Lyman Draper, in his compilation on these events, told of the outcome of the Paint Creek expedition:

Thirty persons volunteered, and started on the last day of the month [August, 1778]; when they reached the Blue Licks, eleven of the number, who had families behind, now began to consider the force too small ...and returned to the fort.

Boone was nothing daunted, for such valiant men as Simon Kenton, Alexander Montgomery, John Holder, Pemberton Rollins, and Jesse Hodges...& heroically persevered. They crossed the Ohio on rafts, and, painted in Indian style, advanced rapidly towards Paint Creek Town.

When within four miles of that place, and Kenton was some distance ahead as a spy, he heard the tinkling of a bell, and soon discovered approaching, an Indian riding on a poney without a bridle, & another Indian skulking along behind, who suddenly bounded upon the horse behind the other with his back to the other, greatly to the rider's surprise, when both set up a loud laugh. Kenton...drew up his rifle and shot, when both fell off, one dead and one wounded, the poney scampering off...

Other Indians hearing the report of the gun & seeing the frightened poney, now advanced ...Kenton sprang aside just in time to see the flash of their guns... He made off... relieved by the rapid advance of Boone and his party, and quite a skirmish ensued... At length the savages gave way... Two of the Indians at least were wounded, and three horses with all the Indian baggage [were] taken. The whites sustained no injury.

This Indian party, which Boone thought numbered thirty warriors, and Kenton estimated at forty, were on their way to join the gathering Indian forces destined against Kentucky...Boone concluded that the expedition against Boonesborough [was underway].

According to Lyman Draper, the men were hesitant to even stop to eat, much less cook, on the return to Boonesborough. They killed a buffalo and stopped to cook it, being very hungry, but the Indians had been posted to watch them. They returned to Kentucky with all possible speed except for Kenton and Montgomery, who delayed their return to get more horses and perhaps a prisoner who could give information.

Boone and his party made a circuitous route back to Boonesborough to avoid the enemy, having discovered them at the Lower Blue Licks. After a hurried return, during which time John Holder developed scald feet, they arrived at Boonesborough on the 6th of September after an absence of seven days. Pemberton Rollins remained with Holder until his feet recovered somewhat and both got in that night or early the next morning.

The Indians were delayed by the need to procure game and were usually late in cooking breakfast. This gave the men and women of Fort Boonesborough time to clean and repair guns, mold bullets, bring in food and fill vessels with water. An anxious night was spent in the fort.

On the British side, Sir Frederick Haldimand, Governor of Canada, received a report from Henry Hamilton, Lieutenant Governor of Detroit:

September 6th 1778

There are at least 400 Indians assembled to attack the fort of Kentucky, where Captain Boone was taken [captured] last year, and several large parties of Indians range the banks of the Ohio...

## Chapter III.

## How-dy, Blackfish

Returning at night, skirting the large body of Indians, the men of the Paint Creek Expedition arrived with news that the Indians would soon approach Boonesborough. By mid-morning next day, September 8, 1778, the women of the fort had finished the early chores and were quilting, perhaps to quiet themselves during anxious waiting. Daniel Boone was outside the fort with his nephews, standing by with rifle in hand as they watered the horses. Moses remembered that he and his brother Isaiah were outside the fort that morning when they saw a long line of mounted men approaching in the distance. Assuming them to be the militia requested from Virginia, they started to run out to meet them. Moses said: "Some thought it was the expected force from Holston". Isaiah told of this first sighting of the Indians:

Moses and Isaiah Boone were out watering some horses, and saw the Indians approaching, strung along very scatteringly, in Indian file, some mounted on horseback, and presented a very lengthy and formidable appearance. Col. Boone was outside the fort at the time, with his rifle, and told the lads to run in, that the people they saw were Indians. The boys had supposed they were the expected reinforcements, and were on the eve of riding out to see them...

Moses described their approach:

...the Indians made their appearance on the hillside south of the fort in Indian file, about four hundred forty, the forty were Canadians, and the four hundred Indians under old Black Fish, some 45 years old.

Estimates of the number of Indians and French or Canadians vary even among those who were present - from three hundred to one thousand. Major William Bailey Smith, then in the fort, said there were six hundred Indians marching in three columns. Their commander was Capt. Duquesne, of Detroit, according to Daniel Bryan. Henry Hamilton said the commander was DeQuindre. [There were three men named DeQuindre, all Lieutenants, on Hamilton's list of "Officers, Interpreters &c" in September, 1778.]

John Gass told:

The Indians made their appearance about ten o'clock in the morning - Black Fish now chief commander, and it was said that there were 300 Indians, 40 Canadians - Capt. Gass does not think [Simon] Girty was along. They struck their flag on the point on the South side of the river, above the fort, a little back from the river - there halted, near a fourth of a mile about 300 yards.

John Gass described the enemy's first approach to the fort:

> Pompey, the negro interpreter, now an Indian, got upon the fence, 150 yards from the fort, and called out to Boone to fulfil his promise - i.e., to surrender up the place, as he had promised the Indians he would. Boone started, and went direct to Pompey...they had two flags but I don't know what they were, whether French or British.

Pompey was known to some in the fort and was heartily disliked. Susan Howell said that the Indians had captured Pompey when he was a small boy. Col. Richard Callaway's granddaughter, Mrs. Richard French, said that "...Pompey wo'd ride up to the fort, and hollow [holler] over (from behind a cabin) 'Capt. Boone, Capt. Blackfish wants to see you'."

Moses continued:

> Col. Boone was outside the fort, with his rifle in his hand, and viewing the Indians, when he was called by his Indian name SHEL-TOW-EE (The Big Turtle)...They gave him a kind reception: wanted him to give up the fort...

Each time the Indians approached the fort to "parley," they brought a white flag signifying peaceful intent. As William Bailey Smith said, "soon another flag came" as the Indians appeared at the fort again. Daniel Bryan, who said he had his information from Daniel Boone, gave a slightly different description of the first meeting with the enemy and mentioned the two flags:

> The[y] came under french & British Coullers. the[y] stuck down their flags when Old Blackfish, the indian commander in Cheaf, the same that formerly had Boon prisoner at Chillicothy, advanced and came within one hundred & fifty yards of the fort where he stopped and called aloud for Capt. Boon. Boon answer him from the fort. He asked Boon to come to him. Boon went to him.

Boone's granddaughter Delinda described the conversation between the Shawnee chief and Daniel Boone:

> On the arrival of the Indian army, Black Fish called for Captain Boon - was he there? "Yes," said Boone, "I am here; I came to prepare the minds of my people to be willing to treat, and surrender."

Boone was explaining in a duplicitous manner why he had run away the previous June from his Indian father, Blackfish. By "treat," Boone meant they would make a treaty.

The following facts, learned "from John South and others," were told by Henry Wilson. (John South was present during the siege.)

> When the Indians appeared, they had a british flag...And seeing the fort newly stockaded, thought it saner to resort to stratagem than ...take it by main force.

Their great father King George didn't want them to kill white men & they had come to treat, & proposed a conference...

The first time the Indians approached the fort and asked for Boone, Daniel Boone went out alone to meet them. He was careful to stay within sight of the fort. In accounts given here, it is said that Pompey or Blackfish, or both, called Boone out. Daniel Boone refused to have the meeting inside the fort as the Indians requested, saying the women and children would be frightened.

Josiah Collins described the first meeting of Daniel Boone and Blackfish:

Blackfish came to the top of a hill...and called to see Boone. Boone and William Bailey
Smith went out. Blackfish said to Boone:

"Well, Boone, How-dy."

"How-dy, Blackfish."

"Well, Boone, what made you run away from me?"

"Why because I wanted to see my wife and children."

"Well, you needn't have run away, if you'd asked me, I'd let you come. Well, Boone, I have come to take your fort. If you will surrender, I will take you all to Chillicothe, and you shall be treated well. If not, I will put all the other prisoners to death, and reserve the young squaws for wives."

Boone said he would return to the fort, and counsel with his warriors.

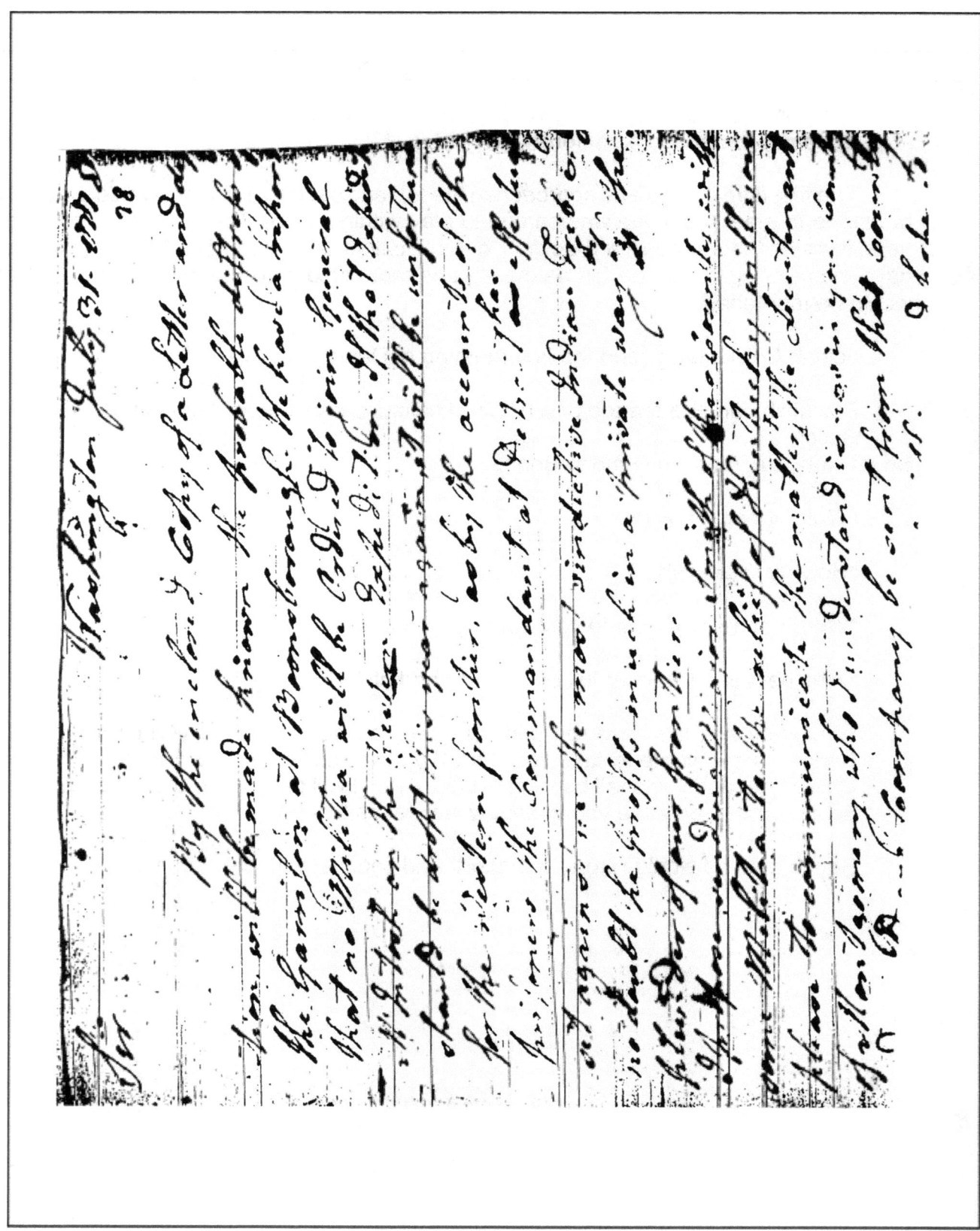

Letter of Arthur Campbell to Col William Fleming. July 31, 1778. DM 4C 78

## *Chapter IV.*

## *To live like Brothers*

Now Blackfish and his adopted son, Daniel Boone, had met for the first time since Boone's escape in June. In an interview with Shane, John Gass told that Boone met with the Indians twice, but there may have been a third meeting on the first day. After the first meeting between Boone and Blackfish, there was a second meeting of Daniel Boone and William Bailey Smith with the Indians. The third would have been later on the first day: the Indians asked Boone to bring out his daughter, Jemima, so they could see her long hair.

For the second meeting, Smith was dressed perhaps as a British officer to back up Boone's statement to the Indians that there were other commanders in the fort and that Boone alone was not able to make the decision to surrender the fort. John Gass told of the first two meetings as he must have heard from Daniel Boone on that day.

> Boone went out and met [the Indians] at the fence as freely & readily I would go to the yard fence. They spread down a blanket up at the head of the lane farther off from the fort. Boone sat down & they gathered round him. Everyone in Fort was then sure that Boone was gone.

> William Bailey Smith went out with Boone the 2nd time to the indian camp, dressed in British clothing - maccaroni hat with an ostrich feather in it &c. Boone said he could discover if he ever went out again he would not get back. He saw it in the indians' eyes...the Indians looked surley ...so [Boone] didn't go out a 3rd time - was dangerous.

Daniel Bryan described the conversation further:

> ...They [Daniel Boone and Chief Blackfish] gave each the hand in a friendly manner when they Enquired how each other had been &c. Blackfish said to Boon My son, what maid you leave us in the Manner you did. Boon answered that he wanted to see his wife and children so bad that [he] could not stay longer. Blackfish said My Son if you had but let me know you wanted to see your wife, he would have let him gone at any time and assisted him in going. He, Backfish, told Boone that the Army which he could then see was sent by the Gouverner at Detroit [Henry Hamilton] to take the inhabitants of Boonsborough prisoners to Detroit.

> He then Shewed Boon a list of wampum, said that it was the orders given to them by the Governir at Detroit to go by - this list of wampum shewed Detroit at one end and Boonsborough at the other end with three lines of beads from one place to the other. On one side a Red Row, in the middle a white row, on the other edge, a black Row or line. The row of red beads was the war path they had come along. The row of white beads was the path they would take back, if his men peaceably surrendered, and the black beads showed they would be put to death if they did

not surrender. This he told Boon was their orders, and that the inhabitents of the fort had it offered to them to be taken on which Row or line they chose.

William Bailey Smith gave an account of the second meeting with the Indians, crediting himself with being in charge. Of Smith, John Gass said he "was no more commander" than anyone else, and "was thought to be fond...of boasting of his services". In Gass's estimation, Daniel Boone was considered the commander during the siege, though there were officers at the fort: Col. Richard Callaway, Captains Daniel Boone, John Holder; David Gass, William Bailey Smith, and perhaps Jacob Starnes may have been a Captain at that time. William Bailey Smith told:

> Three chiefs met them with great parade about fifty yards from the fort, conducted them to the spot designated for their consultation, and spread a panther skin for their seat, while two other Indians held bushes over their heads to protect them from the sun. Here the chief addressed them for about five minutes assuring them of the most friendly disposition, and a part of the men grounded their arms, and advanced to shake hands with them. The chief then produced a letter and proclamation from Governor Hamilton at Detroit, proposing to them the most favourable terms, if they removed thither.
>
> Major Smith replied that the proposition was a kind one, but that it was impossible to effect the removal of all their women and children. The Indian assured him that that was no obstacle, as he had brought forty horses for their accommodation. After a long and apparently friendly consultation, during which they smoked together, and the Indians gave assurances that they had abstained from killing hogs and cattle from a wish not to offend the whites. Major Smith and Colonel Boone returned to make known the proposals and to consult upon the course to be pursued.
>
> On their return, they were accompanied by twenty Indians as far as the limits beyond which it was agreed they should not go. Smith then called together all the men who were within the fort, read to them the letter and enquired what was to be done. They asked his opinion and he frankly told them that the only course he considered judicious and safe was to decline the terms proposed and to resolve to defend the fort against any attack that might be made. The Indians had no cannon, and there was plenty of ammunition within the fort, so that he conceived there was little danger to be apprehended in the result. His counsel was approved and the course resolved on. In a short time the Indians sent another flag in order, as they said, to ascertain the result of the consultation within the fort. Major Smith sent them word that he had told them all he could say on the subject, but if they wished to hold a treaty, as it is called, they must come forward, and a place would be selected for the purpose. Thirty chiefs came forward accordingly, but could not be induced to approach within less than eighty yards of the fort.

The letters from Henry Hamilton which were brought to the second meeting gave the terms of surrender for those in the fort. Moses Boone reported on Hamilton's tactics and described the gift he sent:

Indians now proposed (or perhaps Boone or Smith so proposed) that a Treaty should be made: the Indians to withdraw, and the whites were to abandon Boonesborough and leave the country in six weeks. The Indians sent by Boone and Smith a dozen or more nicely dried buffalo tongues as presents to the women - some of whom felt a little suspicious that it was poisoned, but it was not. This was the first day.

Isaiah explained that the Indians wished the whites to leave Kentucky because "Kentucky was their old hunting ground, and they wanted to preserve it for their own use, and hence desired the whites to leave it."

Lyman Draper said three chiefs were present: Blackfish, Moluntha, and "another chief". Twenty warriors accompanied the chiefs to the second meeting with Daniel Boone and William Bailey Smith.

Henry Wilson told Draper that the Indians intended to take the women and children on horses to the Indian towns, but Isaiah Boone thought the horses were for the trip to Detroit so the men could then fight on the British side in the war. Indeed, British Lieutenant-Governor Henry Hamilton intended to recruit Kentuckians to the British side. Whether Hamilton believed Daniel Boone's promise to surrender the fort is not known, but the Indians probably did believe him. Hamilton offered the Kentuckians the same military rank and the same amount of land as they owned in Kentucky if they became British subjects. Evidently, as John Gass said, the letters and terms were fully discussed within the fort and a majority opinion sought on whether they should surrender.

> I being a boy at that time I did not see the letters but I should suppose they were addressed to Boone. I understand the purpose of the letters was for the fort to give up and they[?] should stand in same Situation in Detroit they stood at ------- Boonesboro.

> [Boone] now left it to the people whether they would go with the indians to Detroit surrender the fort or whether they would hold it out. He wanted to be free from blame should they hold on and the indians overcome them. Boone was blamed for this proposal, but he only meant to shake off responsibility & in going out to make a treaty he did it with the intention of detaining til soldiers came. The idea of the treaty was to detain the indians as long as they could with an expectation of help [militia from Virginia].

No doubt those in the fort remembered another instance of Kentuckians receiving a proposal from Henry Hamilton. A year earlier, Ambrose Gristham was found shot and killed, Hamilton's offer pinned to the front of his coat:

> I assure all such as...take refuge in...any posts commanded by his Majesty's officers shall be humanely treated, shall be lodged and victualled...shall receive pay equal to their former stations in the rebel service and...shall receive his majesty's bounty of two hundred Acres of Land.

Josiah Collins, who said he was "well acquainted" with many of those at Boonesborough, reported a third visit by Pompey to the fort on that first day.

The negro returned the 3d time, the same day, with the message that Blackfish and some of the warriors wanted to see Boone's squaws. Boone returned answer that squaws were very much afraid of the indians. The men at the port-holes would say to the negro not to come any nearer, or they would shoot him. Didn't want him to make any discoveries [that the fort was undermanned].

The Indians were probably curious to see Jemima, Daniel Boone's daughter who had been captured with Betsy and Fanny Callaway two years earlier. Jemima was escorted out to the Indians by her father and Col. Richard Callaway. Her husband, Flanders Callaway, stood guard just inside the fort. Their daughter Susan said:

> ...Finally Indians asked Boone to show them his daughter, about whom he had told them when he was their prisoner. Finally he said he would take her to the gate & show her - Col. Richard Callaway went with her to protect - & several Indians came runing, & wanted to shake hands with her, evidently designing to snatch her off, & use her in extorting terms, but Col. Callaway cocked his rifle, & told them to stand back, cursing them & warning them that he would blow them through if they touched her.

Evisa Coshow also described this meeting of Jemima and the Indians. She said that her grandfather, Flanders Callaway, helped protect Jemima while the Indians looked at her hair. Mrs. Coshow erroneously stated that Mrs. Daniel Boone was also taken out with Jemima, but Mrs. Boone had returned to North Carolina a few months before the siege.

> Grandfather stood inside the gate - they referred to their Squaws wanting to see his Squaws: wanting & begging to see Boone's wife & daughter... then they were brought out of the Block houses to the gate to "how! how!": then they made Signs to see their hair; they took out their combs themselves Showing butefull Suits of hair - let their hair flow over their shoulders...they wanted to get hold of their hair. Boone would stand, and lots of others, ready with the fort-gate comanded with guns...

Susan Howell commented on the treaty talk:

> Col. Callaway then retired with Mrs. Jemima Callaway. Indians had promised if they would come to the gate, & bring Boone's Daughter, & certain whites unarmed, & Indians unarmed, they would shake hands and make peace. Boone then asked for two days to consider the demand to surrender the fort...

During the second meeting, a line had been agreed upon which neither the Indians nor the whites would cross. George Bryan, a Boone cousin, reported that there was one infringement, probably in the early evening of the first day:

> A parcel of young indians came playing around within the limits. Boone pointed to them & complained - Blackfish ordered them off, & they ran & laid down in the corn-field - by where their guns were laying...

Using the extra time gained by asking for another meeting with the Indians, Daniel Boone then put it to the people whether they wished to surrender. John Gass remembered the discussion:

> Boone said he would submit it to the people in the station - if they thought it best to give up, he would yield. Squire Boone said, warmly, he would never give up - would fight till he died. "Well, well," said Daniel Boone, "I'll die with the rest."

> In the Lick, about 60 steps west of the fort...was designated as the most suitable spot to hold the treaty... with the understanding that it should commence next morning. Nothing occurred that night... That comprised events of the first day - 8th September.

Details of the second and third mornings, 9th and 10th of September, are provided in Nathan Boone's interview with Draper. [Some statements have been re-arranged for correct sequence.]

> The following morning Boone again appeared at the old place (within the fire & protection of the fort) & told Black Fish the people had determined not to surrender as long as there was a man living. Black Fish evinced much Surprise and said that they would be very much disappointed - Gov. Hamilton would much regret it - that the Governor had ordered them in case they did not surrender, not to massacre them, and then proposed to hold a friendly treaty, & march home.

> The next day...was the day appointed for the treaty. Black Fish added that he had so many chiefs with him (specifying the number), & they being from so many different towns, would [all] have to participate in the council. Boone said there were a certain number of officers in the fort (more than there really were) & they would have to take part in the treaty, as they could not at once decide, & wished another day to study on it. This was acceded to... The number was less than Black Fish's proposed number of deputies. The green plat in front of the fort was designated for the treaty ground, & the conference then closed.

The Indians were surprised that there would be no surrendering of Boonesborough, as discussed by Daniel Bryan:

> At the expiration of the time alowed them they Returned the answer that they ware determined to hold the fort while a man was left alive, this answer was not Expected by the indians, who then Made one other offer which was that if eight of the leading men in the fort would meet them in council next day, that they would make a lasting peace with them and Return home.
> ...the People in the fort had two Days time given them to Determine whether they would render themselves prisoners or Risk a siege... In this time the women filled all their vessels that would hold water, pails, Buckets, tubs, churns &c all full to

prepare for a siege...& leting all the cattle & horses that came up to the fort insid the fort &c.

The morning of the third day, the people in the fort were wary, Moses said:

That day few or no Indians were seen - kept mostly out of sight: They had held a council the night before - was observed from the fort, had the war dance. This was in the bottom near the hill, and south east of the fort. Col. Boone said this convinced him that the Indians designed an attack; and next morning, when Indians were observed, that that was additional evidence of it.

Col. Boone gave positive orders for the men in the fort to be[?] at their posts, guns in hand and cocked and when treachery should show itself, to fire among the crowd; as the Indians were most numerous, they would be most likely to be the sufferers. The next day Indians quite friendly - Indians got water at spring, and... met some of the women also [there] for water - called them "fine squaws".

Carrying water to the fort was work done by the women, and during the treaty talks it was necessary to stock up on water in case fighting broke out. It would be dangerous to be outside the fort during any fighting. Jemima may have made a sloppy job with her bucket if done as Evisa Coshow stated:

Well I remember hearing my grandmother say that they had to go out of the fort to get drinking water. She said that they could go without being molested. [The Indians would not bother them.] They would rest[?] while dipping it up - then they would fairly fly - She said there would not be much in her bucket when she was let in. This Spring was some two or three hundred yards out side the fort she said...

Pompey continued to approach the fort, tempting its sharpshooters. Moses spoke of this, and of the pretence of parading around to convince the Indians that there were many more men in the fort than were actually there:

Pompey that day rode up two different times on [an] old pony and wanted to swap it for a gun - no one felt disposed to make a trade - no guns to spare, and in any event [not] for him: There was ill feeling towards Pompey, the negro...now was quite efficient [Draper said "officious"] and some of the men declared if he came again, they would shoot him and let the fight commence if it would.

This day, too, the Indians sent word for the women and children not to be alarmed, that they were going to kill some beef - and without further asking or notice, killed several. That day, too, in order to make a great show of strength, the women in the fort put on hats, coats, &c and had guns and marching to and fro in front of the big gate, then open...

Daniel Trabue also described the deception, but said the women marched back and forth upon the roofs of the cabins rather than before the big gate:

[Col. Callaway]...told them for the women to put on hats & hunting shirts & to appear as men & to get up on the top of the walls & thus appear as a great many men; the women did so, & the other men in the fort did also get on the walls & cabins, & showed to a good advantage.

As the day of the final treaty talk began, John Gass remembered that even the cattle seemed to be aware of the suspense.

That morning the cattle were around the fort, uneasy - the Indians were told that the "white squaws" were afraid to venture out to milk, and the Indians aided in driving the cattle into the fort, some 60 head in all. The people of the fort was to get them in for sustenance during the siege - and once there, they kept them...

All told in the fort, negroes included, were 60 - 40 only good, effective [fighting men].

The morning was spent preparing the dinner for those participating in the treaty talk. The treaty spot was sixty yards south from the fort gate, under some trees according to Isaiah, and within gunshot according to Henry Wilson. Squire Boone's sons told of getting the dinner ready. Moses remembered:

The third day in the forenoon preparing for dinner, tables fixed by driving forks in ground and placing slabs on - meats cooked, seats in some manner prepared - intended only for the leading men, those who took part in the treaty.

Isaiah, then age 6, told Draper that he had helped:

...the dinner was prepared, and pretty well prepared - table taken out, and chairs also Isaiah Boone took out one chair himself, small as he was - and dishes, knives, and forks, to make a great show of plenty - to show the Indians that they had abundance of provisions for a siege.

John Gass remembered that the dinner was "the very best that could be provided, and all the tables, chairs, pewter dishes sent out, to give the Indians as good in entertainment as possible." Another young fellow in the fort helped at the treaty. According to Jesse Daniel, Sam South said that he carried water out during the treaty talks.

Two of those present, John Gass and Isaiah Boone, remembered differently about an arbor at the treaty site. Perhaps another arbor was described by Isaiah Boone, who said it was part of the Indian encampment. The arbor described by Isaiah was one in which the tops were cut off a nursery of peach trees, the trunks then used for posts; poles were laid across the top of the posts and the tree branches placed over the poles for covering, and "this was their camp", according to Isaiah. Henry Wilson was not present, but he described an arbor made for the treaty talk, and gave the terms of the treaty:

In the meantime Boone had two benches brought out, & an arbor formed of four poles upright, with sticks across the top with bushes overhead - & a little fire kindled to light the pipe of peace - all within gun shot of the fort & about midway between it and the Indian encampment. Here the treaty was made to continue as long as water should run down Kentucky river - that both should have the right to hunt, & no robbing of hunting camp nor stealing of horses - but live as brothers.

The "treaty commissioners" were selected by the people of Boonesborough. Even the eyewitnesses disagree on who they were. The women of the fort were said to have protested sending out all the "best men;" therefore, some of the leading men remained in the fort for protection during the treaty talk. A clerk was selected to write the articles of agreement. Daniel Bryan commented on the choosing of men who would conduct the treaty talks. [His statements have been arranged to appear in sequence.]

...the garrison... chose Daniel Boon, Squire Boon, Edward Bradley, Daniel Wilcocks, Pemberton Rollins and three others now forgotten their name who went into the council; the place where they held their treaty was about sixty yards from the fort gate under the shade of some large[?] trees that stood in the edge of the Lick within fifteen yards of a high clay Bank that wold shelter them from the fire from the fort. Here seats were Made to set on.

...they all met at the appointed place and seated in the following manner - one white man and two indians untill all the white men were seated on the front seat and sixteen indians; on the back seat, one indian behind every white man, all the indians that were [on the] back seat had concealed a tomahawk under his Match coat, that if any white man was likely to make his escape to tommahawk him...

...after they had seated themselves Blackfish the indian Chief Rose and made this inquiry: Brethren, by what othority did you come and settle this place. he was answered that Colo Richard Henderson had made a purchase of all the Lands on the south side of the Kentucky River to the Cumberland from the cherokee indians and paid them for the same. Blackfish then turned to a Cherokee indian that was Standing and asked him did your People sell this land to the white People? the cherokee answered "Yes we did." Blackfish made a little pause, then turning himself to the white men and said, friends and Brothers as you have purchased this land from the cherokees and paid for it - it entirely alters the case. you must have it and we must live like friends and brothers. Hereafter you must alow us to hunt on your Ground and you must hunt on our side the River thus we are willing to Make a peace with you as long as the Wood grows and water runs - this Agreed to, Blackfish said that there was indians in that Army from twenty four Different towns and that their must be one indian from Every town to sine the articles or the indians of that town wood not consider the treaty binding on them. This brought twenty four indians into council and eight white men - and that they would all meet at the same place on the Morrow and Ratify and sign the articles. when all agreed to, the white men went into the fort and the indians to their Camps.

...in the morning before the white man had left the fort, Boon had given orders that all the men in the fort should be on the watch seated at every convenient place with his Rifle in his hand, presented and cocked, his finger at the triger, and if the

**Squire Boone**
From a crayon portrait presented to the Filson Club in 1886
by Reuben T. Durrett

Indians offered to mist---the whites, to fire at the bulk. that "they would be liker to hit an Indian than a white man, three to one".

Draper recorded what John Gass said:

The treaty commenced. Daniel Boone, Squire Boone, Col. Callaway, Maj. W. B. Smith, old John South, Edward Bradley, and three others (neither David Gass, my informant's father, nor John Martin were of these three), and 18 Indians, Black Fish one, and this conference lasted about midday. All went on well. The Indians were to go off and leave the place unmolested, the Boonesborough people agreeing to become subject to the British Governor of Detroit.

In case the outcome of the treaty was not peaceful, Moses said that plans were made beforehand so that marksmen in the fort were well-organized and alert:

Col. Boone had ordered the men who went to the treaty, as they could not take out their guns, to place them loaded where they could conveniently seize them as they should enter the fort - well persuaded, as he was the ultimate result of the affairs. But it was decided best to carry out the treaty matter, hoping it might end well - and moreover time would be gained, a consideration of greatest moment, as the Holston men were more certainly expected - & every pains were taken to ward off treachery...

The Indians also had made preparations before the final meeting. Daniel Bryan said that the day before some Indians hid "their guns, war equipage and concealed them behind fence logs...&c in order that they could pick them up more handy..."

The treaty talk would have included the passing of the peace pipe. The Boone family avoided tobacco; evidently the Indians knew this. Delinda Craig mentioned "Kin-ni-ke-nick", which was a mixture of dried leaves from various plants such as sumac and sometimes tobacco which was used for smoking by American Indians. Delinda said, "At this treaty they had pipes and tobacco and smoked but Boone could not use tobacco, and they also had kin-ni-ke-nick...and he took a few whiffs."

Mrs. Nathan Boone said the pipe-smoking was not done according to ritual during this meeting, arousing Daniel Boone's suspicion:

Boone discovered & pointed out some Indians at the treaty who had no business there. Met the Indians smoking the pipe & not handing it according to the present custom of peace to the whites to smoke, was another evidence on the part of Boone that the Indians had... premeditated mischief.

Daniel Boone was also suspicious about the added number of Indians as mentioned by Delinda:

Boone discovered Indians' heads exposed from behind trees, and logs, & bushes, and asked Black Fish what it meant - that he had kept his men in the Fort as he had agreed - that it was not acting honorable; that he ought to have kept the Indians away.

Black Fish was truly one of Nature's noblemen - was ordinarily rigidly exact in fulfilling his engagements, yet on an important occasion like this, he deemed it proper and politic to take every advantage. Black Fish said to Boone nothing was designed; they were young men, and curious to witness the details and ceremonies of a treaty.

Black Fish then said, as he, Boone, was a great Captain, two Indians must shake hands with him - he and another - Boone replied that he was no more than any other man, & there ought to be only equal numbers.

During the conference, Squire Boone took advantage of the Indians' awe of a fearsome adversary to report that an army under command of General George Rogers Clark was on the march from Virginia, which was not entirely true, but which caused some uneasiness among the Indians.

John Gass told of the last moments of the treaty talk:

The dinner was eaten - Black Fish now said but one thing remained to be done - he said he must go on to the point of the hill, and speak to his people and tell them a treaty had been done. There he took a position and spoke some time in his own language in a very loud and impassioned manner, addressing his warriors at some distance off - who were not to be seen during the treaty. Having concluded his address to them, he turned to Boone and his eight companions, and cautioned them "not to be alarmed - for when they were truly friends they took as near their heart as they could".

Terms were discussed at the end of the dinner, as remembered by Moses:

The dinner eaten - furniture taken to the fort: Then the peace pipe passed around. This arrangement was ratified...the Indians to leave the country, and the whites, in six weeks to leave Boonesborough. Then Black Fish mounted himself on a stump or bench, and said he would "give out the big talk, that all his young men around might know that a firm peace was made". This was the substance of what he said, mentioning the treaty agreed on. Col. Boone knew what was said, and Black Fish spoke with such a knowledge: He had a fine voice, and presented much of the natural and eloquent orator.

John Gass said that Blackfish "addressed the indians in a voice like old preacher Vardeman's". [Jeremiah Vardeman was a Baptist preacher in Kentucky.] He contradicted Moses Boone's statement that Boone understood the speech given by Blackfish and described the special handclasp which sealed the treaty:

Neither Boon nor any one else understood what he said. He [Blackfish] now came back to confirm the treaty. Told the whites they must not be alarmed, when they were very loving, they took as near the heart as they could.

When the Indians "took near the heart," they grasped the white men above the elbow, a "longer" handshake symbolizing a lasting treaty, Henry Wilson said. Perhaps not just a ruse, the special handshake was described as the way of recognizing a great warrior by an officer during the Revolutionary War. Witnessing the handshake at a treaty involving George Rogers Clark's men and the Shawnee Indians in 1786, Ebenezer Denny told in his Military Journal of an Indian's reaction to finding himself in the presence of George Rogers Clark:

> ...discovered General Clark, and knowing him to be a great warrior, rose and saluted him very significantly - instead of taking hold of each other's hands, they gripped nearly at the shoulder, and shook the left hand underneath the right arms.

But the "long handshake" of Blackfish was seen as the beginning of the suspected treachery. Daniel Bryan commented:

> Black Fish then told Boone that his crossing of the palms of the hands as in shaking of hands was a short grip, which was a short friendship. But that this putting their other hand around the arm below the shoulders was a long peace and that theirs was to continue...

Evisa Coshow wrote to Draper that Daniel Boone knew the special handshake was a strategy:
> No! No! Boone too smart for that - sly dogs, they wanted [to] get 2 hold of them... Boone told them "no, no"... Boone's object was to coax them to Peace. This was trecherous meanness of course - that's what my Grandmother taught me about them.

Daniel Bryan described the final moments of the treaty talk:

> They were all seated and concluded their treaty - when they had concluded and finished their treaty, Blackfish Rose and bid them all stand up. he said unto them, Brethren, we have made a long and lasting treaty so long as wood grow and water Runs. Now we will shake long hands, taking hold of Boon's arm near the sholder, ordering all to take hold in the same manner when all got fixed in that manner, gave the word go.

> [Black Fish] then endeavored after getting them to rise and shake hands in this manner to rush them under the bank. Just at this time, those in the fort fired and put them all in confusion; so that all of the men got away.

> Boone was aimed at by one of the Indians behind him, but the tomahawk went over his head as he was in a bending position, overreaching him and striking him only with the handle. Squire Boone was shot through the shoulder - all others escaped.

According to Lyman Draper, this was the same tomahawk, a pipe-tomahawk, which had just been smoked as the peace pipe.

At the moment of the two-to-one handshake, firing commenced, and Mrs. Nathan Boone said Indians appeared from everywhere: "rose up from behind stumps, logs, rails &c

in every direction, & took part". The siege had begun. The first moments of the battle were described by John Gass, who told that the first shot was fired by the Indians:

> And while Black Fish and another were accordingly embracing Daniel Boone and two Indians each of the others, an Indian at a little distance rose up from his hiding place and fired into the air a signal gun, which he had secreted under his blanket.

> The indians had been ambuscaded [hidden, ready to attack] the night before and when the lst man took hold, the signal gun fired and the others jumped to - and then the indians poured a fire on the fort, to keep those in the fort from coming out to the rescue of those at the treaty.

Moses said that neither party was allowed to bring arms to the treaty and others said the signal gun was fired from a point further away, not by an Indian at the treaty. Susan Howell had heard that the signal gun was "not much louder than a pop gun".

William Bailey Smith said that he himself ordered twenty-five men to be stationed in a bastion in case the treaty did not have a peaceful outcome. Others said the men were stationed at random throughout the fort, even on the roof, and still others told that Daniel Boone had stationed certain men to command each bastion. William Bailey Smith told that when it came time to sign the treaty, Blackfish removed himself from the treaty site to speak to some young men at a distance, and that he "substituted some young warriors...for older men" at the treaty, explaining that the younger men wished it so. William Bailey Smith said he gave the signal for the men in the fort to start firing by waving his hat.

Daniel Trabue, whose account of events at Boonesborough seems biased in favor of Col. Callaway, said that Callaway was in charge, and had ordered the firing to begin:

> ...while the men and Indeans was a scuffling the men from the fort agreable to Col. Calliway's Orders fired on them. They had a drdful skuffil but our men all got in the fort safe. And the fire continued on boath sides after that.

And John Gass told that:

> Boone and his companions were instantly grappled, and [the Indians] attempted to drag them behind the point of the hill where they would be secured from the fire of the fort. All got loose, and ran for the fort.

The treaty commissioners, not armed for the talks, had stacked their guns just inside the fort gate ready for the treachery to begin. They depended on firing from the fort to protect them as they ran to safety. Just one man retained by the enemy would have meant a hostage situation which could force surrender.

## Chapter V.

## *Flash after flash*

Daniel Bryan gave his version of the first few minutes of the fighting:

[Each Indian] started to drag his man behind the clay Bank where they could murder them without being in danger from the fort; but the watch on the fort wall that moment poured unexpected to them so heavy a volley of Rifle shot amongst them that the indians were so confused that the[y] lost their hold and every white man extricated himself and all got safe into the fort except Squire Boon, who Received a ball through his shoulder. The indians flew to their arms where they had concealed them and the battle began like claps of thunder...

John Gass said that "at the first firing Pemberton Rollins had his arm broken above the elbow." Moses told of the escape to the fort and described the wounds suffered by Daniel and Squire Boone:

The Indians seemed to have designed to pull and drag the men into some ditches or guts, where they would be secure. Finally one Bradley [Edward Bradley], an old man, came very near being hauled into one of the guts by a whirl which staggered him, but he got off. Col. Boone received a blow between his shoulders with the pipe end of the tomahawk, which made considerably of a bruise: He thought the aim was to storm him, and take him prisoner, else the blow would have been with the tomahawk's edge. Squire Boone when some 15 paces from the council table, was shot. The ball grazed one shoulder, knocked off some of the ----- back bone, and lodging in the other shoulder. He fell, partly on the fort side of a small hickory tree, but instantly jumped up and ran for the gate. The others had got in, and the gate was shut, and he got in through a cabin out-door, between the gate and south-west corner.

Daniel and Squire Boone's escape into the fort was described by John:

Daniel Boone was the first to get clear. Squire Boone was shot in his flight to the fort, through the back of the neck just above the shoulders. It had been previously arranged that those in the fort should keep a good look out at the porthole, and fire at the mass at the first show of treachery. Those in the fort did fire - and a large body of the Indians seated all around were on every hand, and opened a heavy fire, and when the whites got into the fort, there was no cessation of the firing - kept up pretty warmly the remainder of that day, and all that night...

Daniel Boone's wound was attended by daughter Jemima, according to Susan Howell:

...as Col. Boone got close to the fort gate ...an Indian...aimed a tomahawk blow at Col. Boone, who (unarmed) made a bending attitude to pitch headfirst at the

Indian's legs to throw him, & received the tomahawk blow (tomahawk turned in the fellow's hand) flat sided, between Boone's shoulders, making a bruise, & causing him to spit some blood; & Boone caught the Indian by the legs & gave the fellow a severe tumble & he fell heavily, Boone darted into the fort.

Isaiah Boone thought John South and Squire Boone were the last to get away, and disagreed with his brother Moses:

At the Treaty, old man South [not Edward Bradley, as Moses Boone says] - fat and fleshy, came near being hauled into one of the ditches a few yards south of the treaty spot, by three or four Indians - but he managed to get away.

Three Indians seized hold of Squire Boone, but he easily loosed himself from them... ran a few steps when he received a wound, as described by Moses Boone, which shot knocked him down. He immediately recovered and ran for the fort - the gate being shut, and all in, save himself and South, they both got in at a cabin door, which had previously been designated in case any should be delayed till after the gate was shut.

Isaiah told of his father's injury:

When Squire Boone got into the fort - took his place in the south-west bastion, where [William] Stafford was, which had been assigned to his command in case of an attack, shot his gun, & in re-loading, found his shoulder hurt him...at this moment Daniel Boone came into that bastion, going about to see how the different parts of the fort were getting along, & pushed down the bullet for his brother & as he was a man of few words, did not say much about his wound. Shortly after Daniel Boone cut out the bullet.

Enoch told how the injury was treated:

Squire the last who ran [away from the Indians], and when about halfway to the fort he was shot in one shoulder, and the ball lodged in the other; and as the big gate had been closed as the others were in, he shot his gun, and got in at a private gate - halfway down, when his arms failed him. After a little, Daniel Boone came in and cut out the ball and Mrs. Squire Boone dressed it, & he was unable to take any part during the siege.

Lyman Draper's account includes the statement that Squire Boone's wife "was his only surgeon in all such cases", but in this instance, the skills of his brother Daniel were required.

Simon Kenton, interviewed by John N. James, said he had heard the following from Daniel Boone himself, which contradicts William Bailey Smith's and Daniel Trabue's accounts.

He [Daniel Boone] told me it was his pointed orders to the men he had stationed in the two basteens to shoot without one moments delay and with good aim at the enemy.

Not only were men stationed in the bastions which faced the treaty site, they were well organized with commanders in each group, as revealed by Isaiah Boone's statements. Also, Isaiah told who fired the first shot from the fort:

> When the signal gun was fired, and the Indians seized the whites, the incident of Stafford occurred...Stafford had his eye on his [gun] sight, and taking good aim at the Indian's breast sitting and looking on, so decorated with silver trinkets - and Stafford's gun was acknowledged to have been the first gun fired after the enemy's signal - the Indian fell over dead, thought to have been of some inconvenience from his dress, etc., and lay there till night.

Susan Howell said that Daniel Boone's wound forced him to rest for a time:

> ...thought it was a slight flesh wound; but when he loosened & removed the stock, the blood spurted out so as to alarm Mrs. Callaway [Jemima]; but it was bandaged & checked, & Col. Boone was persuaded to remain partially quiet awhile - by lying down on a bed in his cabin.

> ...he had a porthole made close by, through which he frequently shot as he lay - Mrs. [Jemima] Callaway loading his gun for him. The Indians at length, not hearing Col. Boone's well known voice, called out with a rough curse - "we know we have killed Captain Boone...we haven't heard anything from him for a long time".

> "No, you have not - I am here, ready for you red rascals", Boone would respond.

Serena said that Flanders Callaway had the little finger of his left hand shot off as he ran into the fort. Neither of the Howells remembered that Jemima had been lightly struck by a spent bullet, but the story was told by others. According to a Bryan cousin, George, Jemima Boone Callaway must have been watching for the "treachery" to begin as she opened the gate, and a moment later, one man found the big gate closed:

> ...as they returned to the fort Mima Callaway, Boone's 2nd daughter, as she saw them run - threw open the fort gate, & a ball from the other side of the river, struck the fort gate, bounced against the back of her neck so hard that it knocked her down.

> Jacob Starnes told me they pressed him so hard, he had to run round the fort, on to the other side of the fort next to the river - got in at a small gate.

Josiah Collins corroborated George Bryan's statement that Jacob Starnes was one of the treaty men:

> Jacob Starnes was one that went out to the treaty. An indian grabbed him by the arm. He got away from him, and another indian ran before him, in the way to the fort. The 2nd he knocked down and jumped over him, and so made his escape.

All the men were now in the fort, most running through the main gate where Jemima Callaway may have been stationed to open it for the rushing men. Moses Boone told that when the firing started, one of the younger men in the fort, Ambrose Coffee, was lying on the fort roof. He was warned to get down, but did not. When he did retreat, unhurt, he counted fourteen bullet holes in his clothes.

**Flanders Callaway from Columbus of the West**

## Chapter VI.

## I ish a potter!

Among the inhabitants at Fort Boonesborough was a potter named Matthias Prock; he was called Tice. Moses Boone said Tice was much frightened when the fighting broke out:

During the first alarm, one Matthias Prock, a Dutchman, probably living in Col. Callaway's family, run under the bed at Col. Callaway's, and Mrs. Callaway took the broom stick and punched out and told him to go and fight. He ran out and into Squire Boone's gunsmith shop adjoining and crept under the bellows. Mrs. C. drove him out of this, when he ran and jumped into the new well, somewhere near the old well, which he had probably been digging &c. Prock said, "Sure, I was not made to fight - I ish a potter!"

John Gass explained how Tice Prock found a safe place for the duration of the siege and of his come-uppance with the Callaways afterward:

...Tice in great alarm ran under the bellows in the blacksmith shop. The good and courageous Mrs Callaway, who while she chidingly rebuked the profane, had no sympathy or pity for the coward, finding the terrified Dutchman so ingloriously skulking from his duty, whipped him out of his hiding place with a switch. Poor Tice confessed[?] in a very penetential way his mortal fear of gun powder -"Be sure," said he, "I was not born for a fighter; I was designed for a potter, as I am". But he promised no amends - indeed his cowardice seemed a constitutional failing; and finding he would do nothing towards defending the fort, Col. Callaway set him to digging in the new well, and he worked rapidly so long as he was in the least exposed to the fire of the Indians...

Col. Callaway saw that since he would not fight, he should work. The Dutchman intimated that he would not; whereupon the Colonel drew his tomahawk, which he always carried in his belt, gave chase, and Prock, true to principles of non-resistance, betook himself to his heels and made for the well and jumped down to the bottom at a single leap, some ten or twelve feet deep; and never came out till the siege was over.

Shortly after the siege, Col. Callaway's fine horse was missing; a long and vigilant search was instituted without success, and finally some one happened to take a peep into an unfinished well; and there, to his astonishment, was the lost horse, safe and sound... Passage was dug down, and the prisoner released. The old Dutchman was mightily pleased to think that Col. Callaway had as he said been come up with for making him dig the well.

The fear of the fort inhabitants and the cowardice of Tice Prock were also mentioned by Delinda:

Col. Boone said he thought the people generally felt timid at the commencement of the attack, but it soon wore off; but that Prock was always so, never could fight.

John Gass said that the night before the final treaty talk, the Indians had scattered flax along a fence running to the fort, which they set on fire, probably the first night of the battle. Several men "crept out of the fort, and threw the fence down..."

One of Col. Callaway's granddaughters, Mrs. French, said the women were put in the center of the fort for protection:

> All the women were gathered into a house that was in the center of the fort. The cattle that were in the fort, whenever there was a firing, would run round; and the women, children would be put in the uttermost confusion.

"At the first alarm, Indians firing and yelling, the cattle run around, dogs barked," Isaiah said. The commotion at the fort was observed by the two members of the Paint Creek Expedition who had delayed their return to steal more horses. Simon Kenton and Alexander Montgomery arrived a day later to find the Indians already encamped at Boonesborough. They tried to get into the fort on a foggy night to lend two more sharpshooters to the small force within the fort, but were forced to remain outside. Also outside the fort, William Patton had just returned from a hunting trip to find the battle raging. (Lyman Draper said Patton returned at night on Thursday, September 17th.) He watched from a hill overlooking the battle and from the cries and commotion, assumed that Boonesborough was defeated. He then warned those at Logan's Station to prepare for the worst; if Boonesborough fell, all the Kentucky forts could be taken.

Nathan Boone said:

> "The attack on the Fort was now general and open. The Indians made a rush towards
> the fort, as though they designed to attempt scaling the pickets... They shot arrows and flaming splinters on the cabins and poured volleys from their guns..."

Squire Boone's youngest son, Enoch, who was a toddler at the time of the siege, had heard the story of the Indian who appeared early on in the fighting, and who was called "False Face":

> At the commencement of the fight, an Indian had posted himself behind a log... [wearing] a false face... which he raised and ...several shots were fired at it. When [William] Stafford, suspecting the trick - for after the Indian had pushed up the false face...then he would move [?] himself up and fire, dodge back and resort to the false face again. So after some one fired at the false face other Indians rose up as usual, Stafford quickly fired, the Indian fell to rise no more. When the false face was found after the siege, a number of ball holes were found through it...Stafford...saw him from 1785 to '88 - & Stafford told about his shooting at the false face Indian. Stafford was greatly thought of - very patient, & very obliging.

Another incident which occurred during the fighting was described by Moses:

One man, [Daniel Trabue said this was John Holder] of strong frame, threw stones over the cabin and down the hill. Those below would curse and swear and ask them "to come out and fight like men, and not try to kill them with stones like children". Old Mrs. South (a simple-hearted woman) begged the men "for God's sake not to throw stones; it would make the Indians mad." This became a byword among them and subject of jeer and ridicule.

Several persons told of an Indian cavorting "in bravado". Evisa Coshow's colorful accounts in letters to Lyman Draper included a description [not entirely factual] of this Indian:

...He [Daniel Boone] made at a deep copper colored Buck Supposed to be a Chief - far distant on a Hill: they all had been trying to get him during the siege; he would come out - Slap himself, cut all sort of gymnastic capers, get behind his tree again; all the best marked Shots had tried - So Grandfather [Daniel Boone, not Flanders Callaway] said he would try Old Belzabub, his gun [others say his gun was "Tick Licker"]: he said it was not long until the Indian made his appearance - Said he took deliberate aim - [the Indian] slapped himself and yelled as a demon... half fell in behind the large birch tree - half exposed to sight.

John Gass told of the same incident:

Above the fort and on the same shore lay the trunk of a large sycamore, behind which an Indian posted himself, and there remained nearly the whole siege, and was so fixed that he could shoot without exposing himself...

The Indian was mentioned by Serena Howell:

A very tall Indian behind a tree would step out to show himself in bravado, dodge back before he thought they could shoot him. Finally Colonel Boone, Flanders Callaway & several others by Col. Boone's direction, had their guns elevated - some higher, some lower - & by signal, the next time the tall fellow ventured out, they all fired simultaneously, & he fell to the ground, & lay there all day dead, his body partly behind the tree. In the following night, the Indians removed his body. Couldn't tell which one killed him.

Richard P. Holder told the same story, crediting William Hays with killing the Indian:

...a number of Indians collected on the river bank opposite and after firing ineffectually for a length of time commenced making sport of those in the fort, and one Indian more [than] the rest made a great noise hollowing to them in fort when Hays I think called for his gun just then ----Indian has his back to the fort, stoop down & patted his backside [in] derision of Hays who had threatened to go to the Indian and chastise him with switches. The Indian was in that position when the gun was handed to Hays who fired...the Indian rolled some 40 or 50 yards down the hill when other Indians ran down to him, caught him by the arms and dragged him back to the top and all disappeared and not come again to the same place.

On the third night of the siege the Indians were determined to set fire to the fort; it was the most intense fighting of the siege, and gunfire continued all night. Isaiah described how those in the fort were able to stay out of view of Indians firing into the fort:

> It being unsafe to expose themselves in the fort lest they should be wounded... the people cut doors from cabin to cabin as they adjoined - and thus could go all around the fort without being exposed.

Nathan Boone said the Indians tried repeatedly to "fire" the fort but the roofs were slanted inward which prevented the intended disaster:

> The Indians made frequent attempts to fire the fort by night, by carrying the fire concealed under a blanket - & several in that way got killed. Also attempted to set the fort on fire, by shooting torches on their arrows. But the roofs of nearly all the houses forming the wall of the fort being so constructed, - the shingle roof sloping within the fort, that the torches could easily be removed by sweeping them off with poles.

Lyman Draper described the torches used as weapons by the Indians:

> They would collect the long, dry, loose bark of the shell-bark hickory, with small splints and sometimes flax, well nibbed with dampened powder, and tie the whole around a stick, which served for a handle, with the end of the torch or faggot left loose, and set on fire; and with these the enemy would approach the fort as near as they would dare...from behind some tree or the river bank, would aim to hurl them upon the roofs of the cabins. They were almost invariably hurled with such force that they would pass entirely over the cabins into the fort...

> These torches were well-calculated to produce mischief, prepared as they were with much care, and from such combustible materials, and were a foot and a half or two feet in length, and five or six inches in thickness.

The flaming arrows lit with punk (dry, crumbly wood used for tinder) failed to set the fort on fire, John Gass said, although they were forced to use drastic measures (and, as he described, some drastic language):

> ...on one occasion a torch fell down at the side of an outside door. [This was Henderson's house; Henderson was not there.] The shingles on fire were knocked loose. Were pinned to wooden laths with wooden pins. [John] Holder seized a bucket of water and dashed out the blazing faggot which threatened danger... It had blazed up as high as the top of the house above the top of the door. Capt Holder swore hard. Mrs. Callaway told him it would be more becoming to pray than to sware. Holder swore it was no time to pray then...

This was the only instance that promised any hope of success by their night attempts to fire the fort by torches. One day, however, the Indians shot an arrow with some powder tied in a rag and fastened the point with some lighted punk attached. It lodged on the roof of a cabin and stuck fast, the powder flashed and set the adjoining shingles on fire. Seeing this, the Indians raised a joyous shout; and at once commenced firing at the spot to deter the men from venturing there to extinguish it. The shingles were fastened on but lightly with wooden pins, (fortunate circumstance) and all they had to do was to knock them loose with a stick from within, and they would slide down harmlessly to the ground. The Indians were evidently disappointed with their repeated failures to fire the fort.

Squirt guns, devised by Squire Boone, addressed this threat, said Moses:

During the siege, Indians would shoot arrows, some with burning faggots attached, designed to fire the cabin roofs. A few old musket barrels, unbreeched, were provided with swabs to use to put out fire, and would force out a pint or quart of water at a time upon the roof; and several times were effectually used in extinguishing the fire.

Daniel Bryan described tactics used with the fire arrows:

They blackguarded considerably during the siege... the Indians would fire volleys at the same spot to deter the besieged from going there to put [the fire] out - but they did extinguish it in every instance - and finally compelled the Indians to raise the siege.

Stephen Cooper said the fire arrows poured onto the cabin roofs, and then, rain:

The Indians shot arrows on the cabin roofs, & set them on fire; the whites with squirt guns endeavored to extinguish the fire - this was the third day after the commencement of the attack. Then fortunately it commenced raining...

On this third night, two men in the fort were shot. John Gass told of the first fatality:

On the third night of the siege (the night of the 11$^{th}$ Sept), was the severest firing nearly all night on both sides now flash after flash, and comingled reports of fire and so light that the smallest article could be seen in every part of the fort. One Bundun was shot through the forehead, survived in a speechless condition till the following night, when he died.

Nathan's wife, Olive, said David Bundun died three days later:

Bundun, the Dutchman, died 3 days after receiving his wound at the port hole, in his forehead - & by rocking his body on his elbows & knees seemed[?] by the action to work out his brains from the wound: & that his wife would consolingly remark - "It vas a Gots plessing that the pall didn't hit 'im in de eye".

A second fatality occurred the same night. John Gass told how it happened:

During the night an Indian crept up to within fifteen steps [of] the fort, and tried, near the corner where the fence had been burned the preceding night, whereupon London, a negro of Col. Henderson's, and a real soldier, in order to get a good shot improvidently crept into the passage under the kitchen, and was himself shot in the neck dead...it was a chance shot...

Daniel Bryan told of London's cabin being set on fire:

The black man...had a little garden adjoining the fort, the fence of which joined his cabin on the corner. They set fire to the fence, but the men got inside the floor of the cabin and dug till with a forked stick they could shove the fence away. So it burned out.

As the night wore on, John Gass said, the fire arrows and shooting continued, but at length Daniel Boone called for a temporary cease-fire, "A little before day Boone called out to the men to cease firing - it was a waste of powder... The people in the fort ceased - so did the Indians."

Squire Boone's wife was quoted by her son Isaiah as saying that even at night, it was very light "enough so to pick up a pin from the flashing of guns".

## Chapter VII.

## *Pour it to them, Billy, the day is a-rolling*

The women of the fort, besides parading around in men's clothing to deceive the Indians, taking care of the wounded and children, and fetching water within gunshot of the Indians, also helped with the ammunition when it began to run low. Mrs. Dixon, a Callaway descendant, said, "Elizabeth Callaway and the other Girls melted all the pewter Spoons, Plates, &c for bullets."

W. D. Holder said this of a Miss or Mrs. McGuire:

... recollects to have heard repeatedly...that the Callaway girls moulded bullets at the Fort at Boonesborough whilst the men were discharging them at the Indians and the young ladies themselves repeatedly fired at the Indians themselves...

Jemima's relatives told of her part in the siege. The following was related by Evisa Coshow:

Mrs. Jemima Callaway said she ran many bullets - would take them in her apron when too hot to handle, & distribute them... I think I told you before of hearing her tell of her and the girls and women going out after night, gitting down on their knees, scraping the bullets in their aprons to mold and knick them to use over the next day. She said when they would strike the front, they would flatten in many shapes...Spent balls would strike the fort and patter-pall.

She also aided in putting out the fired roofs... The women would dress in men's clothes, & parade & walk around to make an increased show of numbers. Grandmother said they fought nine days & Nights.

Draper's note explains patter-pall: "light powder loads...would patter on the walls and fall harmless to the ground from long distance firing..."

Jemima's children and grandchildren did not recall her being wounded, but her brother Nathan did:

During the siege, Jemima Boone standing in the door (then must have been married) ...received a spent ball in the fleshy part of her back - and being then only with her underclothes & petticoat on, the ball itself & the part of the linen which it struck was partly ----- with the ball in the flesh, & was easily pulled, as the cloth was not broken by the ball.

Others told of the bravery of the women of the fort, among them Ephraim McLain as he recalled Mrs. Hancock's remark to "Billy" [William Hancock]:

Billy Hancock was on the stairs firing at the Indians - & his old lady [Molly Hancock] had been running bullets for three days and nights was so overcome with fatigue that she fell asleep holding her hands to her face, and her elbows on her knees and exclaimed, though asleep, "Pour it to them Billy, the day is a rolling".

Members of the Cooper family told that their relatives, Molly and Ruth Hancock, participated in the siege:

Molly Hancock, wife of William Hancock, used to carry an iron pan-handle - some five or six feet in length, as her weapon of defence, slept with it in her hands during the siege and after. Ruth Hancock was 13 years old when she went to Boonesboro. She was there in the Big Siege...Mr. Cooper had the facts about the siege from his mother, Ruth Hancock Cooper, who was then in Boonesboro.

**Keziah Callaway**
**Courtesy of the Winchester - Clark County Public Library**

## Chapter VIII.

## Blow them all to h--l

Squire Boone's flagstaff topped by the weathervane in the form of a little gun became a target for the enemy, said Isaiah:

The flag at the head of a tall staff some 40 or 50 feet high, became from the first a mark for the Indians and after several days, they finally cut off with their bullets the small stem just below the flag, and made a great rejoicing when the flag fell. The men soon had the pole down, the flag replaced, and again floating. And now, in time raised the huzza-huzza. The Indians remained quiet at this, and did not seem to try to shoot it down again.

Using his blacksmith skills, Squire Boone, perhaps with Col. Callaway's help, made a wooden cannon; the firing of this cannon was mentioned by several persons. It was probably the first cannon fired in Kentucky. Moses told of his father's cannon:

Prior to the siege Squire Boone made a wooden cannon of tough black gum, and iron-banded: it was tried, and cracked. He made another, and tried it twice and answered as very good purpose. About the 2nd or 3rd day of the attack, this was brought and fired and sent a swivel ball over 200 yards out of the big gate - no particular mark. This now showed a slight crack, and was abandoned. The Indians seemed to suspect its quality - for they hollowed out "fire your wooden gun again".

Daniel added this:

...seeing several Indians sitting on the fence, Squire Boone loaded his hooped black-gum cannon with about twenty rifle balls - fired, it bursted - the Indians at first scampered, finally returned and yelled out "Fire your d----d cannon again!"

And Daniel Trabue stated:

This cannon was fired the second time and burstd. The last time it was fired was at a grop of Indeans at a Distance and it made them skamper perdiously. Whether they was hit with the bullits or whether it was the big loud Report it was uncertain, but one thing is a fact they never was seen in gropes [groups] right after that time.

In an interview with Lyman Draper, Samuel Millard may have heard Squire Boone talking about his cannon:

During the siege the Indians made breast works of rails within gun-shot of the fort, which somewhat taxed their ingenuity; but said Squire, "they must be removed.

And soon, continued he, "I had my wooden cannon made, and well bound with iron, and while I charged, my brother opened a sufficient hole in the pickets through which I fired my cannon, and O Lord! how I made the rails and Indians fly!"

A few days into the siege, those in the fort noticed a "silty" appearance of the Kentucky River from dirt being thrown into it. Because of the steep river bank, they could not see what the Indians were doing, but surmised that they were trying to tunnel into the fort. Daniel Trabue said the tunnel "was the project of a Canadian Frenchman, or was thought", considering it unlikely the Indians would have thought of it on their own. Nathan Boone said those in the fort called out to ask the Indians what they were doing. The reply was "digging a hole, to blow them all to h--l."

Evisa Coshow remembered hearing that it was Daniel Boone who informed them of the tunnel; she told of the counter- measure, a tunnel begun inside the fort:

... I remember her [Jemima] telling us after the siege [began] at Boonesbourgh, Boone came in telling them the savages were trying to undermine the fort. He kept eye on the river discovering the water muddy below the Garrison. Boone ordered Deep trenches dug to counteract their designs. Boone ordered the Dirt they dug in Front to be cast over the Walls in their sight - so they soon quit their underground work.

This "skeem", as Daniel Bryan put it, was nearly successful:

They also tried one other skeem to undermine the fort and got within fifteen feet of the fort wall; the whites discovered their attempt by the River being Muddy below; they then dug a ditch inside their cabbens so wide and deep that a man could stand in it. They kept sintinals in the ditch to watch & listen so as to kill them when they got in the ditch &c. the indians suspected what the whites were doing from seeing the dirt thrown out of the howses...

William Cradlebaugh became irate watching the tunnel-diggers, and attempted an unusual retaliation. This was told by William Nelson, whose grandfather Edward participated in the siege.

William Cradlebaugh hearing the French and Indians undermining at the river [working on the tunnel from the river to the fort], threw buffalo bones over the fort picketing at them. They cussed back - and said the people in the fort must be getting out of ammunition when they had to resort to throwing bones.

Pompey appeared frequently at the tunnel, as told by John Gass:

Pompey came to the place when they had dug into the bank, and put his head up 2 or 3 times. Some of the men shot, while others, set to watch, could see the bullit strike the water. William Collins, a first rate marksman, held his gun cocked and waiting; and when Pompey put his head up again, he fired. That time, no splashing in the water was seen. Pompey was not heard of any more.

Expecting that Pompey had been killed - a very important personage withal, with the Indians - the men would jeeringly call out -"where's Pompey?" The Indians would reply, in broken English, "Gone hog hunting," and sometimes say "Pompey nappo" - sleeping.

Others in the fort reported to Draper that Daniel Boone or William Hancock killed Pompey. Neither Boone's nor Hancock's relatives ever heard them say so.

[Note: The Shawnee words for "asleep" and "dead" are similar. *The Military Journal of Ebenezer Denny* contains a glossary of Indian words learned from the Grenadier Squaw, a Shawnee woman at Fort Finney, Kentucky in 1786. She was the sister of Cornstalk. The word for dead is given as "nepowa". The word for sleep is "nepaywah". Some of the pioneers said "nappoo" meant asleep. The white men could have mistaken what the Indians were telling them, or the Indians could have tried to confuse the matter of what had happened to Pompey.]

The people in the fort were much alarmed by the tunnel, which was some four or five feet high and as wide, extending twenty to twenty-five feet into the river bank toward the fort. They wondered how the Indians intended to use it, according to Moses Boone:

> It became a matter of much conjecture as to this design of the enemy - not knowing how extensive it might be as there were so many whites among the enemy: It was thought that they might dig a wide enough passage to march a large body into the fort, or to place a magazine of powder under and blowing up the fort.
>
> To counteract this, a ditch was dug inside the fort, under several of the cabins on the river side of the fort, some 20 feet long, some 8 feet deep and 3 or 4 feet wide. The rains of nights caused this outside ditch to cave in, and it was abandoned by the enemy.

Daniel Trabue said the Indians and whites nearly met in the middle of their respective tunnels:

> ...The Indians & our men did almost meet under the fort a digging; they could hear one another digging; & when the Indians heard that, they then quit, supposing our people might or would put their big gun there.

John Gass said the Indians did get within ten feet of the fort wall, but the intention was not to use the tunnel to blow up the fort:

...it was generally believed it was their intention when they had gotten near the fort, to break a hole through the ground, and to set...poles and rails up against the bottom of the fort, and so to set the fort on fire, instead of blowing it up.

Efforts to get a view from within the fort were described by Nathan:

A battery was erected in Henderson's kitchen, some 6 feet high and raised to the roof in order to observe what the enemy were doing and also to dislodge them. But this did not answer the purpose nor did the other plan, the ditch or hole dug in the Henderson kitchen. When the counteracting ditch was digging, by Boone's orders, within the fort, & the enemy discovered it, they asked what they were digging? Replied, they were digging a hole to bury them all in.

This retort from the fort was reported by Nathan Boone's wife, "Dig on - we'll dig & meet you...make a hole to bury 500 of you yellow sons of bitches." The taunts on both sides continued until near the end of the battle as John Gass said, "The Indians carried on a great deal of blackguarding and tantalizing, but towards the close of the siege, they seemed to get out of heart and said but little."

Simon Kenton, who heard it from the Indians and one of the Frenchmen present at the siege, gave this statement to John James about the tunnel inside the fort:

[Daniel Boone] commenced digging in the blockhouse, and dug out the whole floor to the depth of four feet. We could have killed any numbers of men who could have entered from a mine. Drewyer, [one of the French commanders] and the indians also, told me that their plan was broken in... by wet weather, & they quit on this account, and not because Boone was digging.

Even the livestock showed the effects of the long battle, said John Gass:

During the whole siege the cattle had nothing to eat, and became extremely gaunt, and even the water given them was but a scanty supply. Occasionally the Indians, from the hill on the north side of the river (which was the shortest shot), and the hills beyond the lick, would shoot into the fort ------ killed a few cattle and horses - and of nights the people would dress the beef they killed, and poor as it was, make food of it.

The suffering of the cattle was reported by Keziah Callaway's granddaughter, Mrs. Richard French, who said "when the siege at Boonesborough was over, the cattle could scarcely low, so high punished for want of water".

## Chapter IX.

## *Providentially, the rain fell*

"I don't believe there was a night that it didn't rain or mist," said John Gass. The rain filled in low places within the fort walls, providing water for the animals, as remembered by Daniel Bryan. John told of the many benefits of the rain which fell during the siege, as recorded in an interview with Draper:

> By a seemingly providential interposition, there were showers almost every night of the siege, which had a tendency [to] keep the roofs so dampened as to make it no easy matter to fire the fort by sending of the fiery missiles upon them. One night towards the close of the siege, a very heavy rain caused large bodies of earth to cave into the subterranean passage [the tunnel], and thus put an end to this scheme, whatever it may have been.

Moses Boone reported the optimism of those in the fort:

> During the siege (except for the first day of the attack, until they saw the Indians could be repulsed, and kept out of the fort) - the men kept in fine spirits, and enjoyed themselves finely. Almost every night, providentially, the rain fell, which wet the cabin roofs and made them the more difficult to set on fire - and water was thus caught for the cattle and for use in the fort. Thus necessity did not wage the completion of the new well; and the old one, though streams were low, furnished water for drinking and cooking.

John Gass said "...the Indians did not all leave at once but gradually, and the firing consequently slackened until on the morning of the twelfth day from their first appearance - i.e., the 20th Sept, when all disappeared."

Someone told Lyman Draper that the last of the Indians to leave was a party of about thirty thought to have been Cherokees. Lyman Draper gave Daniel Boone's estimate of the number of Indians killed as thirty-seven, and a "great number" wounded.

John Gass's account continues:

> They left none of their dead - blood was found in many places where the beleaguered recollected to have had good shots. The Indians left behind several poles and rails[?] all covered over with scaly bark and flax made fast [?] which were thought to have been intended to make an aperture at the outer edge of the fort, and stand these large torches up endwise against the fort and then set it on fire.

Nathan Boone thought there were several Indian bodies found around the fort, "A few dead bodies of the enemy were found around the fort - some deposited in rocks & crevices some little distance far off - & yet others at a greater distance."

John Gass thought many Indians were killed, stated that "many pools of blood were afterwards seen".

Moses concurred:

**Climax of the Treaty**
**Drawn from Historical Data by George W. Ranck**

Several of the men who had thought they had had good shots examined the spots and found signs of blood. Not a dead Indian as found - indeed only one during the whole siege - that that Stafford had killed. The Indians had, as usual, carried off their dead, and most likely thrown them into the river.

John Gass continued:

Bullets were found in great quantities, shot into every part of the fort on every side. The upper bastion next the river, it was thought, had a hundred pounds of lead shot into it. [This was Phelps's, the north-east bastion which Lyman Draper said had been shot at from behind the fallen sycamore tree.]

Within an hour after the Indians had gone, but before the whites knew they had finally left, some of the men went out into an adjoining garden and got a quantity of cabbage and gave more than half to the starved cattle.

Two or three days after the raising of the siege, Kenton and Montgomery came one morning: It was known at Logan's that the Boonesborough people had been besieged; it was feared that all were taken. A few days after [the siege] Capt Dillard arrived from Virginia with a small company of men.

Daniel Trabue told in his journal of the alarm when Patton arrived at Logan's Fort with his mistaken report that Boonesborough had fallen :

William Pattin, who lived at Boonsbourough, was in the woods at the time the Indians came to this Fort; and when he came home the Indians was all round the fort, and he lay in ambush until the siege was almost over. He would go at a distince on some high hill and view the Indians, and sometimes in the night he would approach tolerably near; and on the last night he stayed, the Indians made in the night a Dreadfull attack on the fort. They run up to the fort - a large number of them - with large fire brands or torches and made the Dreadfullest screams and hollowing that could be imagind.

Mr. Pattin thought the Fort was taken. He came to our Fort - to wit, Logan's Fort - and informed us boonsbourough was taken and he actuly Did hear the Indians killing the people in the fort. 'they took it by storm,' he said... He heard the women and Children and men also screaming when the indeans was killing them. We beleaved every word he told us as he was known to the people to be a man of truth.

...Their was great Distress in our fort not only for our selvs but for the people of Boonsborough and in perticular for the 15 Men that belonged to our fort that went their to help them. We thought we was in a Great Perdickament. If the Indeans took Boonsborough with 75 Men what will become of us with only 24? ...We expected every minut to be attaced.

Lyman Draper stated that when Simon Kenton and Alexander Montgomery made their delayed return from the Paint Creek Expedition, new horses in tow, they saw the well-marked Indian trail leading to Boonesborough and thought it best to turn their course toward Logan's Fort. There they heard William Patton's "doleful report", as Draper said, and decided to ride over to Boonesborough to see for themselves and found the fort safely delivered from the enemy.

Moses remembered that one young cow escaped captivity:

The Indians killed several cattle and horses. One young cow, the third day after the siege, came home with a buffalo tug around her horn, some 3 feet dangling, evidently had been taken off by the enemy, and managed to get away & when she got back she capered about and evinced much apparent pleasure at her return.

The relief of the people of Boonesborough shows in Jemima's statement to her granddaughter Evisa, "I remember hearing her Say how glad She was when the treaty was - so she could be free, and garden and not have to be Shut up in a Garrison, so confined - it was joyfull times she said."

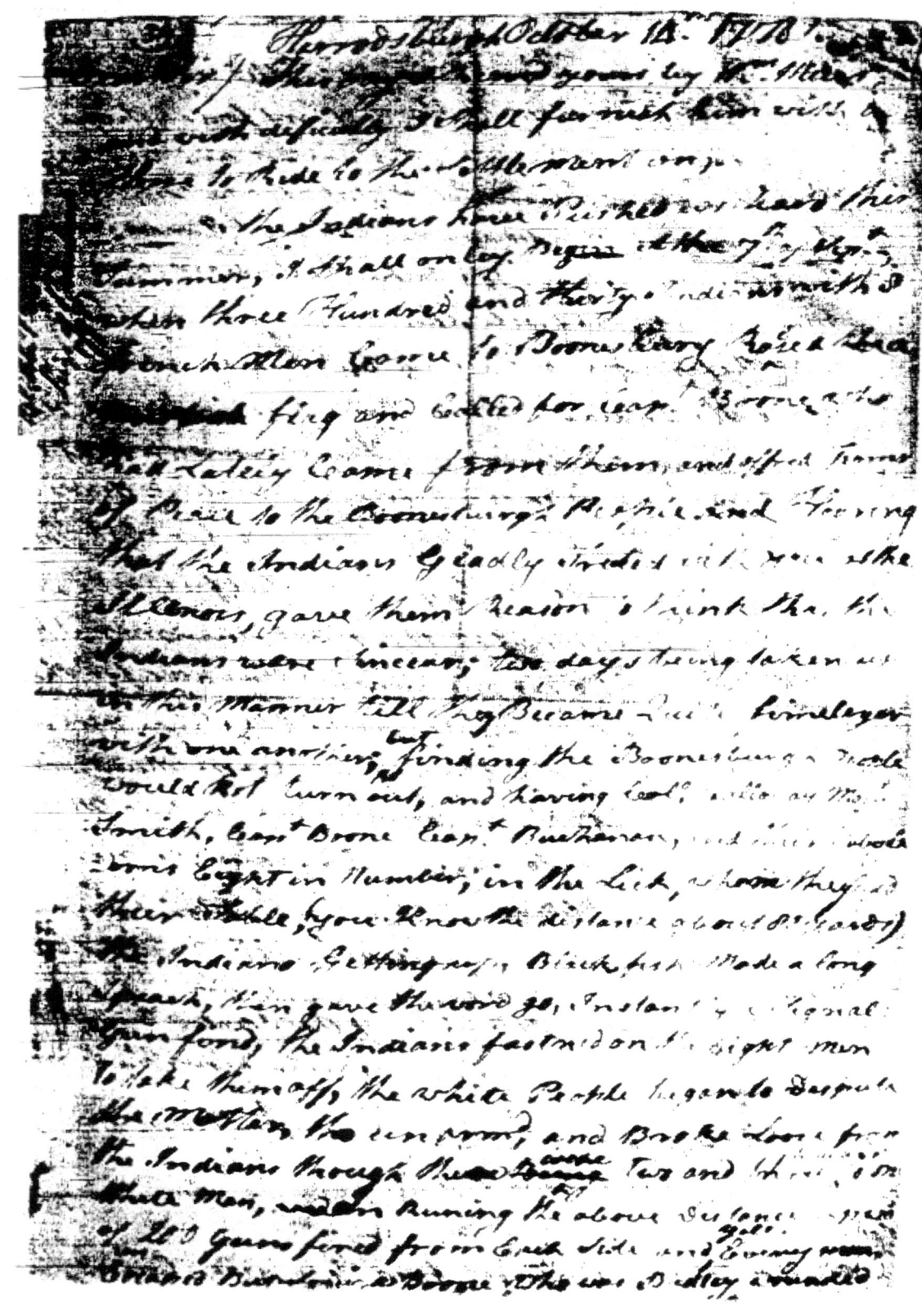

John Bowman's Report of the Siege of Boonesbough. October 14, 1778 DM 48J 42

## *Epilogue*

If the Indians had been successful at Boonesborough, they might have been well satisfied with this single victory, as they had been in taking the saltmakers a few months before. If they had taken Boonesborough, they could have exchanged their prisoners for the bounty offered by Henry Hamilton. Sometimes their prisoners were adopted to replace deceased family members. Encouraged as the Indians might have been by their defeat of Boonesborough, they could have besieged the other Kentucky forts. As Daniel Trabue said, with only twenty-four men, what chance had they at Logan's Fort? Benjamin Briggs told Lyman Draper that Indians did come to Logan's Fort soon after the siege of Boonesborough, but:

> ...made no attack, killed cattle and others came up [to the fort] with arrows sticking in them. There were but 5 horses belonging to the station...they were tied up in the Station - There were 21 guns to defend the Station. They guarded day & night for about 3 weeks, during which time Indians were around & of nights the Indians would come near enough to hollow & laugh & blackguard...

One of the most important decisions made in the fort during the siege was selecting which men would stay inside the fort during the final treaty talk, and which men would go out to parley. The latter were leaders, statesmen in a sense, yet had to be quick enough to get back into the fort if fighting broke out. It was of utmost importance that none of the treaty men be taken hostage or badly wounded as the fort was undermanned to start with. Those stationed in the fort were charged with securing the safety, first of the treaty commissioners, then of the fort in the opening moments of battle while the treaty men joined the ranks of marksmen.

To William Bailey Smith, the crucial point of the siege was the moment the treaty commissioners got away from the Indians:

> The escape of Smith and Boone and their companions at the Indian council was almost miraculous - & can only be accounted for by the confusion into which the Indians were thrown by the prompt, unexpected & destructive fire which poured in upon them by the men in the bastion...the wonderful accuracy of the marksmen avoided although in close contact with them. The rest seeing their comrades unexpectedly fall, had not presence of mind sufficient to prevent the escape of their intended prisoners.

Major Jesse Daniel, when interviewed by Rev. Shane in Montgomery County, Kentucky, evaluated the situation of those in the siege:

> The treaty was in reach of the fort, was an evidence of boldness & firmness - showed they were not easily scared. Went out with a determination not to surrender the fort. It was the nature of Boon, however, to be fool-hardy. The men were under fear - the case was a desperate one. The Indians proposed a treaty...they were willing to risk the getting of a treaty, and to get it thro' any means - if it could be gotten. Men under fear are willing to do anything, if there is a prospect of relief, and desperate cases produce desperate remedies.

The tunnel, potentially a good strategy, may have been the cause of the Indians losing interest in pursuing the siege against Boonesborough. The decision to dig the tunnel was probably made by the French leaders. The Indians did not enjoy this drudgery any more than Daniel Boone enjoyed making repairs to the fort. (He soon found something else to do - the Paint Creek Expedition.) The Indians were never much for manual labor, having their women do that kind of work; they probably would have waged a more fierce battle without the tunnel-digging thought so strategic by French commanders. The Indian manner of fighting was more direct: fire the fort. But even that did not work because of rain and the efficiency of the white men in putting out fires. One white-man's method might have have effected the fall of Boonesborough: cannon. But cannon, or "swivels" as they were called, were not used this year in Kentucky except for Squire Boone's, which so famously "bursted" as Daniel Trabue stated.

George Bryan, who told Shane that he was in North Carolina selling his land at the time of the siege, said that Daniel Boone had attempted to bring cannon to Boonesborough via the Wilderness Road in 1775.

> Boone tried to bring out 2[?] swivels, either when he marked the way [spring of 1775] or brought out his family [fall of 1775], but couldn't get them along. Had to leave them on Yellow Creek 6 miles this side Cumberland Gap. Carried on pack horses. Horses gave out.

The conduct of Daniel Boone from the time he was captured in February, 1778 with his saltmakers until the end of the siege was much talked about. Some considered his offer of February to surrender the fort an act of disloyalty; others thought by offering to do so, he had saved the fort from a winter attack when it would have been taken and the inhabitants massacred or captured. The offer of Boone to 'treat' with the Indians when they came to take the fort in September was also viewed as traitorous by some, while others saw the move as a stalling tactic to wait for military aid from Virginia.

The following statement is from Mr. and Mrs. Richard French.

> Mrs. French always said if it hadn't been for Col. Callaway, the fort would have been surrendered. Boone was willing & [illegible word] to surrender. Mrs. French never could bear an indin's presence.

Members of the Hancock family said that William Hancock at first blamed Boone, thought Boone seemed too cheerful in captivity while he, William Hancock, was so miserable. Afterward William Hancock told relatives that he saw the wisdom of Boone's behavior.

Feelings against Boone ran high. Col. Richard Callaway and others instigated a court-martial of Boone which was held at Logan's Fort. The proceedings were reported by eyewitness Daniel Trabue, who favored the Callaway side of the disagreement. He thought Boone deserved his court-martial, but the outcome was a promotion for Boone.

One of the charges against Boone was surrendering the salt makers, many of whom remained in captivity or were presumed dead at the time of the court-martial. Boone claimed to have used "duplicity". He knew the Indians would be easily appeased by having twenty-six prisoners practically handed to them. They could take all these prisoners and save themselves the trouble of trying to take well-fortified Boonesborough, as Boone explained to the Indians and later at his court-martial. He would surrender it the next summer. Boone's promise to surrender the fort was seen as traitorous by many, and was a focus of the court-martial.

After the court-martial, Daniel Boone returned to North Carolina for a long-awaited visit to his family who were staying with his wife's relatives, the Bryans. Daniel Bryan told of Boone's evident distress at the accusations against him:

> While Boon was gone [captured], his wife and family returned to William Bryan's in North Carolina. Boon wrote to his wife, after the siege at Boonesborough, saying when he would come for her, what had happened &c, and told what Andy Johnson, a little irishman, who was the first that made his escape after the surrender at Blue Licks, was saying viz. that Boone was a tory, and had surrendered to the British and had taken the oath of allegiance to the British at Detroit. Boone said he had not, and "God damn them they [the British] had sent the indians on us".
>
> His wife was then at my father's and I recollect she took the scissors and cut the oath out. Boone was very little addicted to profanity. His allusion was to the scalps being purchased by the British at Detroit.

John N. James interviewed Simon Kenton about 1835, and asked Kenton his opinion of Daniel Boone's conduct at the siege.

> ...with an emphatic nod of the head he replied, "they may say what they please of Daniel Boone, he acted with wisdom in that matter". He was in a poor state of defense, and he wanted to gain time, as he expected succor. The project of the treaty served...the object... Kenton was not present at the siege, but was at Boonesboro very soon afterwards and had the detail from Boone himself - The vigorous truth of his statement is confirmed by the character of Boone as exhibited in all his other conduct.

Whatever was thought of Daniel Boone's behavior in offering to surrender the fort, his ability to get along with the Indians made him the choice for the command during the siege. Many years later in Missouri, Boone gave this advice to a visitor, Maj. Joseph McCormack:

> Always meet them frankly & fearlessly, showing not the slightest sign of fear or trepidation. By kind acts and just treatment, keep on the friendly side of them. Bestow upon the squaws small presents, however short you may be of them, which will conciliate them & secure their good will & friendship against any hostile designs, & command their aid & sympathies in case of sickness while among them...

The expected relief from Virginia arrived at Boonesborough soon after the siege had ended. Three small companies captained by George Adams, John Snoddy and one Hays were commanded by Maj. Daniel Smith, about eighty men in all. They passed Daniel Boone going to North Carolina (after his court-martial) on their journey to Kentucky. While in Kentucky, they expressed interest in going to attack the Indian towns, but Col. Callaway and Benjamin Logan decided it was too late in the year for such an undertaking. The men returned to Virginia.

About a month after the siege, John Bowman reported to George Rogers Clark:

Harrodsburgh October 14 1778

Dear Sir   This Day I received yours by Wm Mu---- and with dificulty I Shall furnish him with a Horse to ride to the Settlement on.

The Indians have Pushed us hard this Summer, and shall only Begin at the 7th Sept - when three Hundred and thirty indians with 8 French men came to Boones burg, Raised a flag and Called for Capt Boone who had Lately come from them, and offer terms of Peace to the boonesburg people, and Hearing That the Indians Gladly Treated with you at the Illinois, gave them Reason to think that the Indians were Sincear; two days being taken up in this manner till they Became quite familiar with one another; but finding the boonesburgh people would not turn out, and having Col. Calloway, Majr. Smith, Capt Boone, Capt Buchanan, and their Subalterns Eight in Number, in the Lick, when they had their Table, (you know the distance about 80 yards) the Indians Getting up, Black fish made a long Speech, then gave the word go, Instantly a Signal gun fired, the Indians fastned on the Eight men to take them off. the white People began to Dispute the Matter, tho unarmd, and Broke Loose from the Indians Though there were two and three Indians to one White Man, --- Running the above Distance upwards of 200 guns fired from Each Side and, Every man Escaped But Squire Boone, who was badly wounded Though not Mortally he got Safe to the fort.  On this a hot Ingagement Insued for nine days and nights, constant fire with out Intermission.

No more damage was Done however But one Killed [this is an error] and two wounded the Indians then Dispersed to the Defents fort whereThey Still Remain in great number and way laying our Hunter - General McIntosh who command[s] the Army against Detroit, and... Received Instructions to strike the Indians and not meddle with Detroit.  For other northern news I refer you to the Gazette I herewith send you.  The Indians have Done more Damage in the Interior Settlements this Summer than ever was Done in one Season before.

NB Pray forward the Newspapers to my Brother after Your Looking over them
              Jno Bowman

  In November after the siege, Nathaniel Henderson filed a petition to the Virginia General Assembly for the loss of his servant, London:

...about the eleventh day of September last...your petitioner had a valuable negro fellow killed.  That the said negro was ordered by the commanding officer to take a gun, and place himself in a dangerous post, & to keep watch and fire on the Indians, which he accordingly did and was killed.  That if the said negro had been suffered to remain within his cabin, he could not have been hurt; That the loss of so valuable a slave, together with the many other losses sustained by your petitioner in that country, distresses him very much.
Therefore hopes that the Assembly will order a recompense, & that the value of the said slave may be paid to your petitioner.

Williamsburg Nov. 21st, 1778.             Nathaniel Henderson

Reporting another event of the months following the siege, John Holder's grandson, Richard P. Holder, said: "my grandfather and grandmother were married something like a year after...were engaged at the time of the siege". This would have been the marriage of John Holder and Fanny Callaway, daughter of Col. Richard Callaway.

Michael Bedinger, the Virginian who came to Boonesborough in 1779, also served in major Revolutionary War battles in the East. His service included the siege of Boston, the siege of Yorktown, service at Staten Island, the battle of Germantown. Later, in his pension statement, he stated his feeling that the service at Boonesborough was more valuable because of "the general distress of the fort." He was "induced...to join Capt. John Holder's company" because of "the feeling of humanity and sympathy for distressed women [and] children..." Of his service at Boonesborough he said, "I have ever considered the service I performed at this place and during this term as the most dangerous, difficult, and at the same time, useful to my country."

There were other sieges and smaller raids against the Kentucky forts during the years 1777 to 1780. A major event occurred in June of 1780 when British advisors led hundreds of Indians in an expedition against George Rogers Clark near today's Louisville. The Indians, afraid of George Rogers Clark, ignored orders of the British leaders and made instead an attack on Licking River at Martin's and Ruddle's Stations. The use of cannon forced a quick surrender at both stations. The result was the massacre of a number of the inhabitants and the near-starvation of hundreds taken prisoner, including women and children, who were forced to walk to Detroit. They remained in captivity for several years.

The year 1782 brought further confrontations with the Indians at some of the newer forts or stations. Estill's Defeat occurred in March when James Estill and his men were defeated by a small party of Indians. The last concerted effort of the British and Indians against a Kentucky fort was the attack on Bryan's Station in August, 1782. The fort held, but the disastrous Battle of Blue Licks followed that siege.

If Boonesborough had fallen, with the other forts as poorly manned as they were, the Indians could have demolished the Kentucky forts and seriously threatened the settlement and defense of Kentucky. Even if the Indians had not actually attacked the other forts, if they had taken only Boonesborough, the other forts would probably have disbanded; at least the women and children would have been sent back east. When the Boone and Callaway girls were captured (and almost immediately rescued) in 1776, the population of the Kentucky forts diminished quickly. Depopulated Kentucky forts, which supplied so many of George Rogers Clark's men, could not have supported his Indian campaigns. When the Revolutionary War ended, there would have been no settlements in "the west"; the boundaries of the western frontier would have receded from Kentucky eastward to Virginia.

Though they were successful in saving their fort, the defenders of Boonesborough, as Lyman Draper called them, were constantly supplying men to other forts under attack. The Kentuckians lived with the fear of siege, which put into the minds of the energetic pioneers that defending might not serve them best. Why not attack the Indians on their home ground? The pioneers saw this as their only hope to stop the raids in Kentucky. When George Rogers Clark called for men (a few months after receiving a petition from the inhabitants of Boonesborough), the besieged Kentuckians were eager to answer as recruits for the coming Indian campaigns. Those pioneers who defended forts and families in Kentucky served bravely and successfully in Indian territory north of the Ohio River. Their efforts, and the efforts of those who followed, secured the Kentucky settlements, while the Indians were pushed further and further away from their homelands and the Kentucky hunting ground.

*Signatures of Some of the Individuals Living at Fort Boonesborough at the Time of the Siege.*

# Sources

Letters and interviews were with or written to Lyman Draper unless otherwise stated. Draper Manuscripts is designated as DM.

CHILTON ALLEN: DM 11CC 54. Shane Interview.

BLAND BALLARD: DM 8J 167 168 [page numbers not consistent, and many words are illegible due to faded ink].

MICHAEL BEDINGER: Dimensions of the fort in *George Michael Bedinger: A Kentucky Pioneer*, by Danske Dandridge, Michie Company Printers, Charlottesville, VA, 1909, p. 38. "I have ever considered" p. 47-8. DM 1A (Bedinger Papers). John Frederick Dorman, Virginia Revolutionary Pensions, VI: 16, Washington, 1958-19--.

DANIEL BOONE: Letter to Col. Arthur Campbell or Evan Shelby ["a copy"]. DM 4C 80.

ENOCH BOONE: Son of Squire Boone. Interview, 1858 in DM 19C 120-153.

ISAIAH BOONE: Son of Squire Boone. Interview 1858 in 19C 57-116. DM 19C 75, 78-86.

JAMES BOONE: Born 1800, eldest son of Nathan Boone and Olive VanBibber, and grandson of Daniel Boone. Interivew. DM 6S 294.

JOHN C. BOONE: Son of Nathan Boone, grandson of Daniel Boone, speaking as Indian Phillips. Letter to Draper. [Ink very faint, some words illegible.] DM 16C 132(5-7).

MOSES BOONE: Son of Squire Boone, nephew of Daniel Boone. Interview Fall of 1846. DM 19C 9-56.

NATHAN BOONE and LADY [Olive VanBibber]: Son and daughter-in-law of Daniel Boone. Interview DM 6S 1-294. 6S 128.

JOHN BOWMAN: Letter to George Rogers Clark. [Two pages are numbered 42. The second is more legible.] DM 48J 42.

BENJAMIN BRIGGS: Interview in Lincoln County, Kentucky, 1844. [Barely legible] DM 9J 183(1).

DANIEL BRYAN: Letters, c.1844, DM 22C 5(13), 5(14), 22C 9(10); "fire your d---d cannon again," DM 22C 10(9); Shane Interview; DM 22C 14; Daniel Bryan's account of the Paint Creek Expedition, DM 22C 5(13).
From DM 22C 5(17) Daniel Bryan's list of those present at the siege and his sources:

...a perticular account of this attack which I have done as near Verbatim as I had it from Colo Boons own mouth. I was not at the seage myself... Rely on the account I have stated...also...accounts...from my Father, Mother and Daniel Boon, Squire Boon, brother to my mother...

GEORGE BRYAN: Brother of Daniel Bryan, DM 22C 16(4), 16(19), 16(22). Shane Interview in DM 22C 16 - 16(25). [Draper's note states that he moved the Daniel and George Bryan interviews from the Shane Papers to his own notebooks in order to keep the Bryan letters and interviews together.]

WILLIAM BUCHANAN: Notes on William Buchanan's deposition from *Petitions of the Early Inhabitants of Kentucky to the General Assembly of Virginia 1769 to 1792*. James Rood Robertson, Louisville, 1914, John P. Morton & CO.

RICHARD CALLAWAY: Richard Callaway's letter with William Hancock's deposition. DM 4C 79.

ARTHUR CAMPBELL: The Kentucky Packet sent addressed to Col. William Fleming, "Botetourt", DM 4C 78 - 80.

CAPTAIN WILL [EMERY]: Shawnee Chief who adopted William Hancock in 1778. Shane interview with Josiah Collins. DM 12CC 105.

THOMAS D. CLARK: Boone Day Speech "Boonesborough - Outpost of the American Westward Movement", *Register of the Kentucky Historical Society*, 72:391-397, 1974.

JOSIAH COLLINS: DM 12CC 64, 74. Shane Interviews.

STEPHEN COOPER: Son of Ruth Hancock, who was in the siege, and grandson of Stephen Hancock. "From Stephen Cooper, son of Sarshall Cooper, near Winters, Yolo County, California, Oct. 16, 1889". DM 11C 98-104.

CORNSTALK: Interview with Thomas Lewis and Charles Clendenin of Mason County, VA - The fathers of both men fought in the Battle of Point Pleasant. Jacob Persinger was named as the former prisoner of the Shawnees who understood what Cornstalk was saying to his men. DM 3S 101 [crossed out] 307. *Memoir of Indian Wars, and Other Occurrences*. [Memoir of John Stuart], ed. Charles A. Stuart. New York Times & Arno Press, reprint 1971 from a copy in The State Historical Society of Wisconsin Library, p. 62

EVISA L. COSHOW: Daughter of Susan Howell, and granddaughter of Jemima Boone Callaway. Letters c. 1889 in DM 21C 24(5), 21C 27, 21C 24(6), 21C 27(1), 21C 24(6), 24(11), 21C 68.

WILLIAM CRADLEBAUGH: Statement about throwing buffalo bones is from William Nelson, grandson of Edward Nelson. DM 18S 230-3.

DELINDA BOONE CRAIG: Daughter of Nathan Boone, and granddaughter of Daniel Boone, born 1801 in St. Louis. DM 30C 56ff.

MAJ. JESSE DANIEL: Shane Interview, Montgomery County, KY [no date]. DM 11CC 94.

MAJ. EBENEZER DENNY: *Military Journal of Ebenezer Denny*, Philadelphia: J. B. Lippincott & Co, 1859; rept: The New York Times and Arno Press, 1971. Handshake, p. 71. Shawnee vocabulary, p. 277.

MRS. DIXON: Samuel H. Dixon's letter taken from his notes of his mother, a granddaughter of Richard Callaway. DM 24C 30(6).

LYMAN COPELAND DRAPER: Draper's account of the June 1778 expedition, DM 4B 178. Draper's account of the Paint Creek Expedition - (August - September 1778), DM 4B 204-209. Draper's own compilation on the siege, DM 4B 202 ff.
Draper's list of those in the siege, 4B 217(1).

Draper's interviews and letters pertaining to the siege were compiled from various portions of the manuscript collection and put together in volume 31C.

Draper's note re: interviewing Daniel and George Bryan and purchasing John D. Shane's papers is quoted in DM 22C 14:

> The following notes of conversations with Daniel Bryan, & George Bryan, were taken about 1844 by Rev. John D. Shane, of Middletown, KY - & afterwards of Cincinnati, O. There he died in or about 1865. At the sale of his books & papers, I purchased all his Ms. notes - & detached these Bryan memorabilia, so as to place them with the Danl. Bryan narrative furnished me by Mr. Bryan in 1843 ["& 44" crossed out]. Mr. D. Bryan died in 1845. I visited him in 1844 & can attest to the candor, reliability & good memory of the man.
> Sept. 10, 1884                                         Lyman C. Draper

[Editor's note: Lyman Draper did not purchase all of the Shane manuscripts; some of Shane's papers are held by the Presbyterian Historical Society, Philadelphia. See *The Shane Manuscript Collection*, William K. Hall, Frontier Press, Galveston, 1990.]

DREWYER / PIERRE DROUILLARD? [Note: "Drewyer" was probably Pierre Drouillard, an Indian interpreter from Detroit.] *Michigan Pioneer Collections* IX: 9, 470, from *The Haldimand Papers*. Pierre Drouillard's name appears as Interpreter for the Hurons on Henry Hamilton's "List of officers, Interpreters &c" in the Indian Department, District of Detroit, on September 5, 1778.

FLAGSTAFF: Isaiah Boone in DM 19C 75.

RICHARD FRENCH and Mrs. French: Richard French was the son of Keziah Callaway French, and grandson of Col. Richard Callaway. Shane Interview. DM 12CC 204-5.

JOHN GASS: Son of Capt. David Gass and Sarah Gass, he was age 14 when he witnessed the siege of Boonesborough. Lyman Draper interviewed John Gass in 1844, the first of three interviews, Shane having interviewed him earlier. Gass and Draper corresponded for about ten years. The last letter from John Gass is dated about two weeks before his death which occurred on 24 December 1855, DM 11CC 10-11. Shane

Interview, quoted in the Anna Turley Noland Papers Vol. 3, p. 238-245. [The Shane Interview in the Kentucky Papers of 11CC is illegible in places, and this transcription was used to fill in the poorer copy.] The Anna Turley Noland Papers are held by Special Collections and Archives at Eastern Kentucky University Library.
DM 24C 74, John Gass, interview with Lyman Draper, Nov. 14, 1844. Statements about Pompey.
DM 24C 100, letter: "Indians looked surley", William Bailey Smith was commander no more than any other.
DM 24C 85, letter, August 9, 1848.
DM 24C 92(1), letter, Oct 24, 1850.
DM 24C 107, letter, January 2, 1855.

AMBROSE GRISTHAM: William Whitley Papers, DM 9CC 7-8-9 (transcription at Kentucky Historical Society).

HENRY HAMILTON: There are at least 400 Indians assembled... Temple Bodley. *George Rogers Clark* I:93, quoting *Michigan Pioneer Collections* IX: 465.
Henry Hamilton's list of "Officers, Interpreters &c" *Michigan Pioneer Collections* vol. IX:470, from the Haldimand Papers.
Hamilton's Proclamation quoted in Dale Van Every: *A Company of Heroes* (William Morrow and Co., New York, 1962), 170-1.

STEPHEN HANCOCK: *Fayette County, Kentucky Records* Volume I: 289, Michael L. Cook, Cook Publications, Evansville, IN. Stephen Hancock's deposition was taken in Madison County, KY on May 23, 1808.

WILLIAM HANCOCK: Richard Callaway's letter with William Hancock's deposition. DM 4C 79.

NATHANIEL HENDERSON: DM 14S 18.

JESSE HODGES: DM 15C 25(13). Pension Statement in DM 1 OO 63, part I.

RICHARD P. HOLDER: Grandson of John Holder. Letter, 1850, DM 24C 29(3).

W. D. HOLDER: Descendant of John Holder. Letter, 1849, DM 24C 27.

MRS. SERENA HOWELL: Wife of Lewis Howell, daughter of Mrs. Fanny Lemme, granddaughter of Flanders & Jemima Callaway, and great granddaughter of Daniel Boone, born in 1806. Interview, DM 23S 239.

SUSAN HOWELL: Born 1791 near Boone's Station, daughter of Jemima Boone and Flanders Callaway, DM 23S 219.

INDIAN PHILLIPS - see John C. Boone.

JOHN N. JAMES: Judge John N. James, notes he took of Gen. Simon Kenton, DM 11C 77.

JUNE EXPEDITION 1778: Lyman Draper's account of this expedition and his list of participants: William Bailey Smith, Capt. David Gass, (Joseph Drake crossed out), Ephraim Drake, John Pleak, [12 crossed out, 13 others. 4B 177-179.

KIN-NI-KE-NICK: Definition from Webster's *New World Dictionary*.

MAJ. JOSEPH McCORMACK: Interview with Draper in Missouri, DM 30C 110.

EPHRAIM McLAIN: [Statements of McLain contain some errors.], DM 16C 7(3).

SAMUEL MILLARD: Interview. DM 21S 252.

WILLIAM NELSON: Grandson of Edward Nelson, interviewed Sept. 8-9, 1863 when William Nelson was age 60, near Boonesborough, KY, DM 18S 230-3.

PLATS OF FORT BOONESBOROUGH
  Lyman Draper stated that he had three plats of the fort drawn by:
    John Gass in 1844, drawn as the fort was in 1778, DM 24C 74(9)
    Moses Boone, drawn as in 1778, DM 19C 12.
    Bland Ballard, drawn as in 1779, DM 8J 167(1). Bland Ballard's sketch
    is poorly microfilmed and almost illegible.
  Lyman Draper himself drew a sketch of the fort "upon the spot" in 1845, DM 11C 78
  Other plats of Fort Boonesborough:
    John Gass sent another plat of the fort with a letter to Draper in 1848, DM 24C 89.
    Josiah Collins, drawn as in 1778 for a Shane interview, DM 12CC 74.
    Richard Henderson's plan, DM 26CC 76
    George W. Stoner, drawn as in 1777, DM 24C 55(5)
  Draper also mentioned "Hall's sketch" [James Hall: *Sketches of History, Life, and Manners in the West. Philadelphia*: 1835. H. Hall. This drawing is the same as Richard Henderson's plan for the fort.]

POUR IT TO THEM, BILLY: Ephraim McLain in a letter of 1884. [There are factual errors in McLain's letters, although he claimed to have heard Daniel Boone and William Hancock tell the stories at Hancock's house in Missouri in 1810 when he was ten years old.] DM 16C 7(3-4).

NICHOLAS PROCTOR: Deposition given "in the Town of Richmond, Madison County on the 14th day of June 1816...in a suit in Chancery in Madison Circuit Court wherein George M. Bedinger is Complainant and Wm. Martin and the heirs of Joel Walker[?] are defendants...", DM 1A 187.

QUILTING: Thomas Bouchelle from Mrs. Jemima Brown's narrative, DM 9C 75.

WILLIAM BAILEY SMITH: *Western Review*. January 1821, DM 30C 87.

SQUIRT GUNS: Devised by Squire Boone, told by Stephen Cooper, DM 11C 98-9; also mentioned by Michael Bedinger and Moses Boone.

JOHN TODD: Letter to Patrick Lockhart, Esq., Botetourt [County] Virginia [John Todd was second in command at St. Asaph's Fort.] *History of Kentucky* I:153. Temple Bodley, Chicago: S.J.Clark, 1928.

DANIEL TRABUE: Narrative of Col. Daniel Trabue, of Adair County, Kentucky. Written in 1827. *Westward Into Kentucky*, edited by Chester Raymond Young, University Press of Kentucky, 1981. Trabue's Narrative also is found in DM 32S 400-427. Corrected spelling appears in Draper's version.

JOSEPH WADE: Joseph Wade was living in Mason County, KY during the 1780's, and interviewed in Ohio by Draper. DM 19S 158.

HENRY WILSON: "Mr. Wilson learned these facts from old John South and others." DM 9J 12. [partly illegible].

## Names of Those in the Fort at Boonesborough During the Siege

This list is drawn from statements of eyewitnesses and their descendants, from depositions, court records, military records, Daniel Bryan's list, Lyman Draper's list, and the editor's research. There are about forty men of fighting age on the list. The usual estimate was forty "effective" men (able to fight) and 60-70 persons altogether, including about fifteen from Logan's Fort who came to help. Even those present during the siege gave contradictory statements about who was there. Ages of participants are supplied when available from pension statements, depositions, etc.

(See the key following this list.)

William Beasley (B) (D) (A-1)
Daniel Boone, age 44. (B) (D) (S)
Israel Boone (D) (A-1)
Jemima Boone - see Callaway
George Boone, brother of Daniel (S-1) (A-1)
Squire Boone, age 38? (D) (S)
Mrs. Squire Boone (Jane Van Cleve), age 28 (S)
    Jonathan Boone, age 12 (E-1)
    Moses Boone, age 9 (S)
    Isaiah Boone, age 6 (S)
    Sarah Boone, age 4 (E-1)
    Enoch Boone, age 1 (E-1)
Edward Bradley (D) (S-2) (T)
John Brian (B) (D) (A-1)
Arabia Brown, age about 28 (E-2)
Claiborn Brown (E-3)
Elizabeth Dooley Brown, about age 21, wife of Arabia (E-4)
"Miss Bryant" (E-5)
William Buchanan (D) (S)
John Bullock (B) (D) (A-1)
David Bundan or Bundrin (D) (S) Killed during siege
Mrs. David Bundan or Bundrin (S)
William Bush (D) (A-1)
Richard Callaway, age 50's (D) (S) (T)
Mrs. Richard Callaway (Elizabeth Jones Hoy), age 45 (D) (S)
    Elizabeth "Betsy" Callaway - see Henderson.
    Frances "Fanny" Callaway, age 15 (E-6)
    Caleb Callaway (E-6)
    Edmund Callaway, age about 14 (E-6)
    Keziah, "Kizzy" or "Cuzzy", age 10 (E-6)
    Lydia Callaway (E-6)
    [John] Jack Callaway, age 3 (E-6)
Flanders Callaway, age 24? (B) (D), nephew of Richard Callaway
James Callaway, age 22? (B) (A-2), nephew of Richard Callaway
Jemima Boone Callaway, age 16 (D) (S), daughter of Daniel Boone, wife of Flanders

John Callaway (B) (D) (A-1)
Jesse Cofer/Copher (D) (A-2)
Ambrose Coffee, age about 19 (D) (S)
William Collins (D) (S-3)
Jesse Conway, age 17 (E-7)
John Conway, age l9 (E-7)
------ Crabtree (D) (S-4) (T?)
William Cradlebaugh, age 25 (B) (D) (S)
Reuben Doblin (B) (D) (A-1)
Dolly, servant of the Callaways (E-8)
Margaret Drake? (E-9)
Ephraim Drake (D) (A-1)
David Gass, age 46 (B) (D) (S) (T) [Daniel Bryan: David "Gess"]
Sarah Gass, age 42 (E-10) Wife of David Gass
    Mary Gass, age 17 (E-10)
    Sarah Gass, age about 11? (E-10)
    John Gass, age 13 or 14. (D) (S)
    Margaret Gass (E-10)
    Jennie Gass, age about 12 (E-10)
    William Gass, age 1 (E-10)
John Gass (D) (S-5) a young man, the nephew of David Gass
Miss Elizabeth Gentry (A-1) (E-11)
Stephen Hancock (B) (D)
    Ruth Hancock, age about 14 (S)
    Cynthia Hancock, daughter of ---- Hancock (E-12)
    Robert Hancock, age 1, son of Stephen (E-12)
William Hancock (B) (D) (S) brother of Stephen
Molly Hancock, wife of William (E-12)
Morris Hancock (D) (E-12)
George Handley (E-13)
John Handley (E-13)
John Hart (E-8)
James Hays (E-14)
William Hays (D) (S) (E-14) son-in-law of Daniel Boone.
Samuel Henderson (D) (E-15)
Elizabeth "Betsy" Callaway Henderson, age 17?, (E-15) daughter of Richard Callaway
Fanny Henderson (E-15), infant daughter of Samuel and Betsy
John Hill (B) (D) (A-1)
Jesse Hodges, age 18 (D) (S-6)
John Holder (D) (S) (T)
Aaron Horn, Sr. (E-16)
Elizabeth Horn, wife of Aaron (E-16)
    Mathias, age under 20 (E-16)
    Aaron Jr., age under 20 (E-16)
    Joseph (E-16)
    Polly - see Proctor (E-16)

# Appendix

    Nancy (E-16)
    William, age under 20 (E-16)
Edward Keadley (D) (A-1) (E-17)
Beal Kelly (A-1) (E-18)
John King (B) (D) (L)
London, age 24 (D) (S) servant of the Henderson family, killed during siege
John Martin (S-7)
William Manifee/Menifee (D) (L)
William Miller (D) (A-1)
Edward Nelson, age 60's? (B) (D) (E-19)
Harriet? Margaret? Nelson, wife of Edward Nelson (E-19)
    John Nelson, father of William (E-19)
    William Nelson, age 1? (E-19)
Moses Nelson (E-19) - brother of Edward?
John Orchard (D) (S-8)
----- ----- [Mrs. George Park] (A-1) (E-20)
William Patton, age 21? (S-9)
George Phelps (E-21)
Josiah Phelps, age about 28 (A-2?) (D) (E-21)
John Phelps, age 33 (E-21)
Lucy Phelps, age 16, sister of Josiah (E-21)
Sam Phelps (E-21) (L?)
Thomas Phelps (D) (A-1)
William Phelps (E-21)
Matthias (Tice) Prock (S)
Benjamin Proctor, age about 25?, son of Nicholas (E-22)
Elizabeth Proctor, age about 10 (E-22)
James Proctor, age about 20?, son of Nicholas Sr (E-22)
John Proctor, age about 20? (E-22)
Joseph Proctor, age about 30? (D) (E-22)
Littlepage Proctor, age about 25? (E-22)
Nannie Proctor?, age 34, 2nd? wife of Nicholas, Sr.? (E-22)
Nicholas Proctor, Sr., age 54? (E-22)
Nicholas Proctor, Jr., age about 30? (L) (E-22)
Polly Horn Proctor, age 19?, wife of Joseph (E-22)
Reuben Proctor, age about 30? (L?) (E-22)
William Proctor, age 5 (E-22)
Mary Ann Proctor, age 1 (E-22)
Pemberton Rawlings/Rollings (B) (D) (S) (T)
George Richardson (A-1) (E-23)
Bartlett Searcy (A-2)
Reuben Searcy (B) (D) (A-1)
Richard Searcy, age 22 (B) (D) (A-1?) (L?)
William Bailey Smith, age 40 (D) (S) (T)
John South, Sr. (D) (S) (T)
John South, Jr. (E-24)

Samuel South, age about 12? (D) (E-24)
William Stafford, age 21, born North Carolina (D) (S-10)
Jacob Starnes (S-11) (T)
Oswell Towns/ Oswald Townsend (B) (D) (A-1) (E-25)
Mrs. Richard Wade (E-26) (S)
Daniel Wilcoxen (B) (D) (A-1) (E-27) (T), Nephew of Daniel and Squire Boone.
Harry ---- (L?)
Tom ----- (L?)

## *French, and Indians at the Siege*

Indian Phillips [John? Phillips] (S)
Blackfish (D) (S)
Black Hoof, Shawnee chief (D)

Jacques Baby (D)
Isadore Chene (D)
Moluntha (D)

## *Key*

A-1   not mentioned in any siege accounts: William Beasley, William Bush, Israel Boone, George Richardson, Miss Gentry, ---- ---- [Mrs. George Park]
A-2   saltmakers on siege lists who were still in captivity: James Callaway, Jesse Copher, Bartlett Searcy
B     Daniel Bryan's list
D     Lyman Copeland Draper's list [he incorporated Daniel Bryan's list]
E     Editor's list
E-1   Squire Boone's children and birthdates were given by Enoch M. Boone, son of Squire Boone and Jane VanCleve. DM 19C 120.
E-2   Arabia Brown - one of Daniel Boone's saltmakers, probably escaped from captivity in spring of 1778. *Virginia/West Virginia Genealogical Data from Revolutionary War Pension and Bounty Land Warrant Records*, Vol. I (Wardell).
E-3   Claiborn Brown - Pension Statement in Dorman: *Virginia Revolutionary Pension Applications* 11:21
E-4   Elizabeth Dooley Brown's marriage date (May, 1778) stated in *Virginia/West Virginia Genealogical Data from Revolutionary War Pension and Bounty Land Warrant Records*, Vol. I (Wardell) suggests that she may have lived at Boonesborough during the siege. Her husband Arabia Brown, was known to have been one of Daniel Boone's saltmakers who escaped a few months after he was captured in February, 1778.
E-5   "Miss Bryant" French Tipton Papers, V:83. [The French Tipton Papers are held by Special Collections and Archives at Eastern Kentucky University.]
E-6   Richard and Elizabeth Callaway's children Edmund Callaway: *Our Kin: Bedford County Virginia Families*, 324, Ackerly and Parker, C. J. Carrier Co., Harrisonburg, VA. Elizabeth's age from her gravestone in Montgomery Co., KY.
E-7   Jesse Conway - Dorman: *Virginia Revolutionary Pension Applications* 22:27-8 .
      John Conway - Dorman: *Virginia Revolutionary Pension Applications* 22:28-30.
E-8   Dolly and/or John Hart are named as siege participants in the following:
      A newspaper account of the 1840 celebration of the founding of Boonesborough in the *Farmer's Chronicle*, William L. Neale, editor, from an original paper belonging to

Judge W. R. Shackelford, Richmond, KY, June 6, 1840 in *Register of the Kentucky State Historical Society*, 1926, 24:175-181.

Article in French Tipton Papers Memorandum Book II: 262 on the Boonesborough Celebration, Saturday, May 23, 1840

E-9   Margaret Drake was probably the widow of Joseph Drake, mentioned in pioneer accounts as having been killed in sight of the fort at Boonesborough in 1778. (John Gass said he was killed at the Starnes massacre which occurred in today's eastern Madison County, KY in spring or summer 1778. John Gass, letter of Nov. 28, 1850 in DM 24C 100.) Margaret Drake could have returned with the Boone family in May, 1778 to North Carolina, but apparently gave birth to a child at Boonesborough in 1779. Margaret Drake may have died in childbirth. The child, Rhoda, was the daughter of John Holder. John Holder and his wife Fanny Callaway reared Rhoda with their children. Family files at Winchester - Clark County, KY Public Library.

E-10  Gass family data from Turley Noland Papers.

E-11  Elizabeth Gentry was named by John H. Brandenburgh, of Madison County, Kentucky in the William H. Miller Unpublished Manuscript, Vol. I, article #180a (no page number). This is the only mention of Elizabeth Gentry's having been at the siege.

E-12  Molly and Ruth Hancock were mentioned by Stephen Cooper, son of Ruth Hancock and Sarshal Cooper, grandson of Stephen Hancock. DM 11C 100. Robert Hancock's birth year is from his letter, 1850, in DM 24C 22(6)

Cynthia Hancock - William H. Miller Unpublished Manuscript Vol. I: 81a.

E-13  Brothers George and John Handley were named in Shane's interview with Mrs. Craycraft. DM 12CC 54.

E-14  James Hays - Septimus Scholl in Shane interview, DM 11CC 51. William Hays had returned from escorting Mrs. Daniel Boone and children and his own wife Susannah back to North Carolina. DM 6S 189, Nathan Boone interview.

E-15  Samuel Henderson, wife Betsy Callaway Henderson, infant daughter Fanny. Lyman Draper's Notes in DM 5B 77-8.

E-16  Aaron Horn - Some of the Horn Family data was provided by Diana C. Frymyer, Irvine KY, descendant.

Family tradition of Proctor descendants say the Proctor family came to Boonesborough with the Horn family. The men of both families were in Capt. Riddle's Company which arrived at Fort Boonesborough in the spring of 1778. It is not known whether the men, when their enlistment was up, returned to North Carolina and brought their families out to Kentucky the same year. Family tradition gives information that both families were present during the siege of Boonesborough.

That Mathias, William, and Aaron Horn Jr. were underage in 1779 is proven from the deposition of Mathias Horn given in a Madison County KY Circuit Court Suit (Elizabeth Horn vs. Christopher Horn et al., June Term 1803). [Suit transcribed by Edward Puckett, copies provided by Kathleen Noland Calder.]

Mathias Horn's Pension Statement - *Estill County, Kentucky and Its People* (Estill County Historical and Genealogical Society, Ravenna, KY 1988), 78-79.

E-17  Edward Keadley in John Gass's letter of 1857. DM 24C 100.

E-18  Beal Kelly said he was a Boonesborough in the fall of 1778, but may have arrived just after the siege, DM 1OO 54, part I.

E-19  William Nelson, grandson of Edward Nelson, DM 18S 230-1. Some Nelson family data is from researcher and descendant Jackie Couture and from the editor's

| | research. Green Clay Papers, University of Kentucky Archives: depositions filed in a suit of Nelson's Heirs vs. Estill's Heirs. Josiah Collins named "Ned Nelson's family" |
|---|---|
| E-20 | ---- ---- [Mrs. George Park] French Tipton Papers, I:81. |
| E-21 | Phelps Family. John Phelps named in Anna Turley Noland Papers: Revolutionary Soldiers of Madison County [KY], p. 7: "John Phelps, born in Virginia about 1745, died in Madison Co KY 1798. He married Katherine ------ and lived at Boonesborough during the siege, helped defend the fort." George Phelps is named in Anna Turley Noland Papers: Revolutionary Soldiers of Madison County [KY], p. 7. William Phelps - John Gass in DM 24C 57(2). Josiah Phelps - named by relatives, but no mention of being at the siege in his pension statement. He stated that he came to Kentucky in 1777 under Capt. Richard May, that he served with George Rogers Clark for three months beginning late June 1778, went to Kaskaskia. Lucy Phelps - siege accounts. Sam Phelps? from Logan's Fort? Daniel Trabue's statement "Sam." |
| E-22 | Proctor Family - Four or five sons of Nicholas Proctor, Sr. came to Kentucky in spring of 1778 with Capt. Riddle's Company. Their father may have been among the militia company, or they might have returned to bring out the family. Proctor information from Kathleen Noland Calder of Irvine, KY, 1998. |
| E-23 | George Richardson Pension statement, DM 11C 41. |
| E-24 | John South, Jr. was the older brother of Samuel South. Lyman Draper presumed that John Gass and Samuel South were about the same age. DM 24C 75(4). Samuel South was in Estill's Defeat, and escaped. Samuel South and John Gass were probably were still in their teens at the time the Indians attacked Estill's Station, and John South Jr. was killed at this time in the battle of Estill's men against the Wyandotte Indians in March, 1782. |
| E-25 | Oswald Townsend gave his pension statement [DM 11C 24] in 1833 in Madison County, Kentucky when he was age 74 before Richard French (son of Keziah Callaway). He stated during the years 1775, 1776, 1777 he acted as a guard for the Fort at Boonesboro and Indian Spy in Boone's company, that he then returned to North Carolina before returning to Kentucky in the 1780s. |
| E-26 | Mrs. Richard Wade [nee Judith Hancock?] from her son John Wade, letter from Alpha, Clinton County, KY, 1861 DM 140(1). |
| E-27 | Daniel Wilcoxen - Daniel Bryan's letter in DM 22C 5(13), DM 1 OO 41, part III. |
| L | Men from Logan's Fort who came to help out were named by Daniel Trabue. |
| S | Persons mentioned more than once in siege accounts and not noticed here. |
| S-1 | George Boone is mentioned in Stephen Cooper's statement in DM 11C 101. Stephen Cooper was a relative of the Hancocks. |
| S-2 | Edward Bradley is mentioned in John Gass's account in DM 24C 73(4), 24C 100, also in accounts of Daniel Bryan and Moses Boone. |
| S-3 | William Collins is mentioned in John Gass's account in DM 11CC 14, a Shane interview. |
| S-4 | ----- Crabtree was not mentioned in siege accounts and John Gass remembered no person named Crabtree who lived at Boonesborough. DM 24C 10. Lyman Draper's account of the siege states that Crabtree was a treaty commissioner and "far surpassed common men in size, strength and action." |
| S-5 | John Gass, nephew of David - mentioned by John Gass, son of David, in DM 24C 100(1). |
| S-6 | Jesse Hodges - his statement that he went on the Paint Creek Expedition. DM 15C 25(13). His statement that he was in the siege: Pension Statement in DM 1 OO 62, part I. |

S-7  John Martin was named by Joseph Jackson who not present at the siege as he was still a captive of the Indians in 1778. DM 11C 60ff. John Gass told Draper in an interview of 1844 that "John Martin made Boonesboro his home before & after the siege of '78 - but don't recollect whether he was there at the siege". DM 24C 74(6).

S-8  John Orchard - Robert Hancock stated it was he who shot the Indian across the river, DM 24C 22(2).

S-9  William Patton returned to the fort while the siege was in progress, watched from a distance, concluded the Indians had won and took this news to Logan's Fort. Daniel Trabue's Journal..

S-10  William Stafford from Isaiah Boone, DM 19C 75.

S-11  Jacob Starnes - George Bryan told Lyman Draper that Jacob Starnes was one of the treaty commissioners: DM 22C 16(19) and 22C 16 (22) Shane Interview. Age and birthplace from *Kentucky Military Pensioners 1818-1840*, The Researchers, Indianapolis, IN, 1985.

T  named as treaty commissioner at the siege

## Boonesborough Residents Not Present During the Siege

Rebecca Bryan Boone, wife of Daniel, had returned to North Carolina thinking her husband dead after being captured by Indians in February, 1778. With her were her children except for Jemima, who was married by that time. They were escorted back to North Carolina by son-in-law William Hays, who also took his own wife, Susanna, back home to North Carolina with her relatives.

William Bush, who had helped build Boonesborough with Daniel Boone in 1775, is not mentioned in any of the siege accounts. He also could have been with George Rogers Clark at Kaskaskia. Bush is on Draper's list of those present during the siege, however.

Green Clay, said to have been at Boonesborough during the siege, came to Kentucky in 1779, according to his deposition in *Fayette County Records*, Vol. I, Cook (p. 92).

Simon Kenton had gone on the Paint Creek Expedition with Boone and others, and had delayed his return to steal horses.

John Martin had resided at Boonesborough, but was at Logan's Fort when word came that the Indians were about to attack. He was sent as "Express" [messenger] to Virginia for help and was gone during the siege. (Some accounts credit him with some sharp-shooting during the siege.)

Michael Stoner is not mentioned in accounts of the siege, although he was known for his scouting and hunting exploits at Boonesborough. He could have been out on a hunt, or perhaps was with Clark at Kaskaskia.

The Saltmakers: several men from Boonesborough were captured by the Indians in February, 1778 while making salt at the Lower Blue Licks. The exact list of saltmakers has not been established, but among those probably still in captivity during the siege were:

| | | |
|---|---|---|
| Samuel Brooks | Micajah Callaway | Benjamin Kelley |
| William Brooks | Jack Dunn | John Morton |
| Arabia Brown | Ansel Goodman | Bartlett Searcy |
| John Brown | William Stagg | William Tracey |
| Nathaniel Bullock | John Halley | Thomas Foote |
| Jesse Cofer | George Hendricks | Richard Wade |
| James Callaway | Joseph Jackson | James Mankins |
| | | Jonathan Ketcham |

## *Families at Fort Boonesborough During the Siege*

The following is additional information found by the editor in conjunction with research for this compilation. The information has not been verified and is offered as presented to Draper and others by the pioneers and their descendants. A list of families is first; a list of men of fighting age follows. There will be some duplications in the two lists. When participation in the siege is questionable, or contradictory statements were given, question marks are used.

### THE DANIEL BOONE FAMILY

Daniel Boone
Jemima Boone Callaway, daughter of Daniel Boone

### THE SQUIRE BOONE FAMILY

Squire Boone
Mrs. Squire Boone. (Jane Van Cleve)
Children of Squire and Jane VanCleve Boone:
Jonathan Boone
Moses Boone
Isaiah Boone
Sarah Boone
Enoch Boone

### BOONE RELATIVES

George Boone, brother of Daniel.
James Hays
William Hays, son-in-law of Daniel Boone.
John Brian
"Miss Bryant"

### THE BROWN FAMILY

Arabia Brown?? - captured with the saltmakers in February, 1778, he said he escaped within a few months and returned to Boonesborough; may have taken part in the siege.
Elizabeth Dooley Brown, wife of Arabia

### THE BUNDAN OR BUNDRIN FAMILY

David Bundan/Bundrin - killed during siege.
Mrs. David Bundan/Bundrin
[The name is spelled "Bundrin" by Lyman Draper, DM 4B 236.]

## THE CALLAWAY FAMILY

Richard Callaway
Mrs. Richard Callaway (Elizabeth Jones Hoy), second wife of Richard Callaway
Col. Richard and Elizabeth Callaway's unmarried children who probably were present at the siege:
Frances "Fanny" Callaway
Keziah "Kizzy", or "Cuzza" Callaway
Edmund Callaway??
Caleb Callaway
Lydia Callaway??
John Callaway, youngest child of Richard Callaway.

## RELATIVES AND SERVANTS OF RICHARD CALLAWAY

Flanders Callaway - nephew of Richard Callaway and husband of Jemima Boone.
John Callaway? - a young man, relative of Richard Callaway
Dolly, servant of the Callaways

## THE DRAKE FAMILY

Margaret Drake?

## THE GASS FAMILY

David Gass
Sarah Gass, wife of David
Children of David and Sarah Gass:
John Gass
David Gass
Mary Gass
Sarah Gass
Margaret Gass?
Jennie Gass
William Gass

John Gass, a young man, the nephew of David Gass. May have been present during the siege, or with George Rogers Clark. He lived at Harrodsburg at least part of the time during the mid 1770's.

## THE HANCOCK FAMILY

William Hancock
Stephen Hancock, brother of William Hancock.
Kitty Hancock, wife of Stephen Hancock?
Mary (Molly) Hancock, wife of William? Hancock.
Ruth Hancock, daughter of Stephen
Cynthia Hancock, daughter of ---- Hancock
Robert Hancock, son of Stephen Hancock.
Morris Hancock, relation to the other Hancocks not known.

## THE HENDERSON FAMILY

Samuel Henderson, brother of Richard Henderson, Proprietor of the Transylvania Company
Elizabeth "Betsy" Callaway Henderson, daughter of Richard Callaway and wife of Samuel Henderson. According to some family letters, Betsy Callaway and Samuel Henderson had returned to North Carolina with their infant daughter in "1778-1779", just after the siege. Others state that they had returned in 1777, before the siege. Lyman Draper's notes state that the Hendersons returned to North Carolina after the siege.
Fanny Henderson, infant daughter of Samuel and Betsy Callaway. This child was said to be the eighth baby born in Kentucky, and the first born to parents who were married in Kentucky. Her birthdate has been given as May 29, 1777. [Facts about Fanny from Society of Descendants of Bowman's Station Settlers Newsletter, v. 3 no. 2.]
London - Negro servant of the Henderson family

## THE HORN FAMILY

Aaron Horn Sr. came to Kentucky in spring of 1778 with Joseph Proctor in a militia company, as stated in the latter's depositions. Family tradition of both families states that the Horn and Proctor families came to Kentucky together, and Elizabeth Horn, widow of Aaron Sr., stated that "she together with her husband in the year 1778 moved to the county and that very shortly thereafter her husband departed this life". Aaron Horn died in late September or early 1778 "at Boonesborough" according to Stephen Hancock's deposition in 1802-1803. [Family information from Diana Frymyer, 1994, and Kathleen Noland Calder, 1998. Madison County, KY Circuit Court Suit, July Term 1803 transcribed by Edward Puckett.]
Elizabeth Horn, wife of Aaron
Aaron, Jr. married Peggy ---
Mathis married Susanna Hall
Joseph
Polly married Joseph Proctor
Nancy married Daniel Dumford
William married Susanna ----

## THE NELSON FAMILY

Edward Nelson Came to Kentucky with Daniel Boone in spring of 1775, and brought his family to Boonesborough later that year. He died about 1788 of the effects of serving on Logan's Campaign in 1786.
Wife of Edward Nelson - French Tipton gave her name as Harriet Morgan, but she is listed as Margaret in court records.
Moses Nelson - born 1758 according to a deposition given for Josiah Collins in Bath Co KY in 1833. Perhaps a brother of Edward Nelson.

## THE PHELPS FAMILY

William Phelps
Josiah Phelps?
John Phelps
Lucy Phelps, sister of Josiah

George Phelps
Thomas Phelps?
Sam Phelps?

## THE SOUTH FAMILY

John South, Sr.
Margaret, wife of John South Sr.
John South, Jr.
Samuel South

Other children of John South and Margaret may have been present at the siege but were not named: William, Benjamin, Weldon, Elizabeth, Sarah, Polly. These children were named in John South's will.

## THE WADE FAMILY

Mrs. Richard Wade (nee Judith Hancock).

## UNKNOWN

These persons were mentioned, but very little information was given about their families or how they happened to be at Boonesborough.

----- ----- - later Mrs. George Park
Miss Elizabeth Gentry, afterward married ----- Bowman

## *Men of Fighting Age Who May Have Participated in the Siege*

William Beasley
Edward Bradley
Claiborn Brown
William Buchanan
John Bullock
David Bundan/ Bundrin
Ambrose Coffee
William Collins
Jesse Conway
John Conway
Sam Phelps?
Matthias (Tice) Prock
Benjamin Proctor?
James Proctor?
John Proctor?
Joseph Proctor?
Littlepage Proctor?

William Cradlebaugh
Reuben Doblin
Ephraim Drake
----- Crabtree
George Handley
John Handley
John Hill
Jesse Hodges
John Holder
Aaron Horn Jr.
Nicholas Proctor Sr?
Nicholas Proctor Jr?
Reuben Proctor?
Pemberton Rawlings/ Rollings
Reuben Searcy
Richard Searcy

Aaron Horn Sr.
Mathis Horn
William Horn
Edward Keadley
Beal Kelly
John King
Jarrett Manifee/Menifee
William Manifee/Menifee
William Miller
John Orchard
William Bailey Smith
William Stafford
Jacob Starnes
?? Daniel Wilcoxen
Harry ----
Tom -----

## French, and Indians at the Siege

The following list is from *American Revolution in the West*, George M. Waller, Nelson-Hall, Chicago, IL, 1976, p. 80;

Indians and others of the opposing side present during the siege: Blackfish, senior chief, Moluntha, Black Hoof, the Chippewa leader, Black Bird, who pledged his loyalty to the Americans. Lt. DeQuindre and the French partisan Chesne (Chene).

The following list is drawn from all sources used in this compilation, including Draper's list:

- Indian Phillips [John? Phillips]
- Blackfish - Shawnee War Chief
- Black Hoof - Shawnee Chief.
- Black Beard [Black Bird] - Chippewa Chief
- Moluntha - Shawnee King after Blackfish was killed.
- Isadore Chene - French-Canadian interpreter for the Wyandots.
- Antoine Dagneaux DeQuindre - French commander from Detroit.
- Duquesne - Though even Lyman Draper listed "Duquesne" as one of the Frenchmen at the siege of Boonesborough, the name was apparently invented by John Filson, perhaps from pioneer usage and/or confusion about French names in general.
- Jacques Baby - fur trader, captain, and interpreter in the department of Indian Affairs.
- Pierre Drouillard - French/Canadian trader.

**Black Hoof. Shawnee Chief**

## Miscellaneous Biographical Data

The following excerpts from the Draper Manuscripts, court records, family files, etc., provide some biographical and other data on a few of the siege participants. No effort has been made to verify statements included here. The statements are chiefly random remarks made by relatives of the pioneers in interviews with Lyman Draper, and/or miscellaneous findings of the compiler. Question marks appear when transcription is not certain.

### BLACK FISH

In the Summer 1779, Col. John Bowman, who was County Lieutenant...of the whole country now the State of Kentucky, Collected and Ordered all the Militia that could be Raised ...in Order to go to take Chellecothy town [Chillicothe, the Indian town]...

[They] attacted the town the Indians were much alarmed & quit the Cabbens & Asembled in a large Council house with their Chief Blackfish...the Indians made port-holes in their Counsil house: the men took possession of their town & commenced a heavy fire on the Council house & killed a Number of the Indians...Blackfish was Constantly Beating a kettle Drum, to Collect the Indians... we Burned all their town except the Council house, killed Blackfish in the Council house, [we] took all the Richest of their plunder and one Hundred & Sixty three Horses, left 6 or 7 brave men dead on the field & Retreated.

James Patton, Lieutenant for Capt. William Harrod, and quoted in Bodley: *History of Kentucky* I: 201 [punctuation added and abbreviations spelled out].

### BLACK HOOF

... was born about 1716 at Eskippakithiki, the "Indian Old Fields" of today in southeastern Clark County [Kentucky]. He rose by sheer force of daring and success as a warrior in battle to be the principal Chief of the Shawnee Nation. His high sense of integrity, superiority of the mind, and some facial features have suggested to not a few that beneath his dark copper coloring he carried a remarkable strain of English blood.

From *Early History of Clark County Kentucky 1675-1824*, Willard Rouse Jilson, Frankfort KY, Robertson Printing Co., 1966, p. 25

"...Tecumseh...like Black Hoof... was a great orator."
Charles Anderson, letter c. 1886, Kuttawa, KY, DM 10J 271

### DANIEL BOONE

Col. Boone was 5' 8" high - broad shoulders and chest and tapered down... His hair was moderately black - eyes blue, skin fair. Teeth very strong and large...

Nathan Boone, Daniel's youngest son, interview, DM 6S ca. page 270 [page numbers illegible].

Commenting on Daniel Boone's Indian name Shel-tow-ee (The Big Turtle):

Quite appropriately named - was about 5 feet 8 inches - high broad shoulders, heavy set, wide under jaw - high retreating forehead - face broad & florid - He also possessed heavy limbs, & nervous & energetic: Blue eye - sandy complexion, light hair...

... Boone was very social - fond of relating past events & had an interesting way in these relations. He had an air of pleasantness about him - fond of mischief... once when a boy, he & Henry Miller took off a man's waggon wheel & put it up on the man's barn - had some spite at him.

In Missouri he was Spanish commandant - both civil & military jurisdiction. - Would take fall hunts.
Moses Boone, nephew of Daniel, DM 19C 1-56.

...five feet 8 or 9 inches high, stout, strong made, light hair, blue eyes, yellow eyebrows, wide mouth, thin lips, fair complexion, nose a little on the Roman order.
Daniel Bryan letter Jan 23, 1843, when he was age 86, DM 22C 5 [punctuation added].

Col. Boone didn't exceed 5'10" - very well set. Well made man. Hair, reddish sandy. Complexion fair. High forehead and hollow eyed, middling long nose and that bowed over a little... of remarkable pleasant temper, nothing appeared to ruffle his mind, or make him uneasy...of a pleasant countenance.
Josiah Collins, Shane interview, DM 12CC 74.

Boone was not a man of talent or information. A ferin [fairing?] good soldier and hospitable. Temperate. Decent man. Not profane.
Cave Johnson, DM 9J 151(1).

Col. Boone - was a member of the Virginia Legislature in Feb. 1781, at Charlottesville, and was captured there & kept one night - & then let go free. Boone could sing well, & while prisoner, seemed to care very little about it & sang for the British.
Israel Morrison, interviewed in Lincoln CO KY in 1844, DM 8J 145(1).

Heard from someone, don't remember whom, that Col. Boone once managed to draw the bullets from the guns of some Indians - & then putting the bullets in his mouth, informed them that he was bullet proof - that they could not harm him by shooting at him. They tried it - he had on a leather apron, in which as they believed he caught the bullets as they shot - he was unharmed, and, as they concluded, under the special protection of the Great Spirit.
Mrs. Nicholson, daughter of Jacob Boone, who was a first cousin to Daniel Boone. Interviewed in Maysville, KY, DM 9S 45.

"Boone himself told me about drawing the bullets from the Indians guns."
Ephraim McLain said he heard Daniel Boone and "Hancock and Mrs. Hancock" tell stories at Hancock's house in the fall of 1810, when he was ten years old. Letter from Little Rock, MO, 1884, DM 16C 8. McLain's letters contain some errors.

The following pertains to the time when Daniel and Rebecca Boone were living in Bourbon County, Kentucky.

> ... He asked how far [away] we lived. Dada told him about 70[?] miles. He said old woman, we must move, they are crowding us. I remember how his wife looked and the dogs, he had six. He had a horse to carry his game on. He had a load of furs ready to take off... He was dressed in leather...I heard him tell dada he liked fish better than any thing else. I could tell you lots about these [other] men but nothing more about Daniel Boone as he did not stay one place long to get acquainted and lived in a world of his own. I have seen him pass with his old horse loaded with game of every kind?. He would go by where we lived and would sometimes talk to Dada and tell what luck he had [hunting]...

Letter of Christopher W---or Mann, Oct. 15, 1888, DM 15C 26, 26(1), 26(2), 27 [punctuation added].

> Grandfather Boone said he had a squaw that claimed him as her buck; he said she mended and dried his leggings, Patched his mockasons...

Evisa L. Coshow, granddaughter of Flanders and Jemima Boone Callaway, DM 21C 63 (3-4).

> In June, 1819, I made a trip of one hundred miles for the purpose of painting the portrait of old Col. Daniel Boone. I had much trouble in finding him. He was living some miles from the main road ...I found that the nearer I got to his dwelling, the less was known of him... A good illustration of the proverb, that a prophet is not without honor save in his own country.
>
> ...I found the object of my search engaged in cooking his dinner. He was lying in his bunk, near the fire, and had a long strip of venison wound around his ramrod, and was busy turning it before a brisk blaze, and using salt and pepper to season his meat.
>
> I at once told him the object of my visit. He hardly understood what I meant...
>
> He was much astonished at the likeness...

From Chester Harding's "Egotistigraphy," DM 16C 56. [In a letter to Lyman Draper, Harding offered to sell a likeness of Daniel Boone to Draper for two hundred dollars.]

The following is a letter of Green Clay, father of abolitionist Cassius M. Clay, to Daniel Boone in Missouri about 1806.

> You and your old lady (who I hope is well) are both old and in a new country where there will of course be many hardships to encounter and could you believe that you are able to travel back to Kentucky, and will come and show the lines, or the corners, or one or two corners and lines of Jacob's two claims or either side of them, I will provide for the support of yourself and lady all your lives afterwards: I will either let you have negroes, or stock, or cash, whichever will be your choice to accept, and which you may think will be agreeable to you two...I know you were very ill treated by many persons for whom you did business, and I also know the great difficulties you labored under and the great distress you suffered by doing business for people who gave you no thanks for you trouble - nor ever[?] paid you your just due. These people ought to suffer...

Nathan Boone told Draper about his father's reaction to this offer:

> But Col. Boone would not consent to go - said that when he left Kentucky, he did it with the intention of never stepping his feet upon Kentucky soil again; and if he was compelled to lose his head on the block, or revisit Kentucky, he would not hesitate to choose the former.

Green Clay to Daniel Boone, DM 6S 219-220.

> In 1809 Kenton went to Missouri, and visited his old friend Colo. Daniel Boone. Reached Boone's just evening - Boone was out some distance skinning a buck. Kenton asked Mrs. Boone for entertainment [lodging] for the night. Mrs. Boone said they had no spare beds & could not keep him. "Why not? - you had better let me stay," continued Kenton. "No - nothing for you to sleep on." "I think," added Kenton, "you would, if you knew who I am." Mrs. Boone now stepped to the door of the cabin where some of the lingering rays of light yet stole in, to get a good look at the stranger; but she said she did not recognize him. "Would you know Simon Butler?" [Kenton's other name] "Yes, but you are not him." -"Yes, I am! - and smiled - and this smile caused her to recognize his old familiar features; she threw away her pipe which she was smoking, & clapped him in her arms, & made so much noise in expressing her joy as to attract Col. Boone's attention, who came in to see the cause. He was quickly told that Simon Butler was before him, when he, too, became joyously excited. All three sat up all night, rehearsing the story of the olden time & the varied fortunes of their ancient companions in the early settlement of Kentucky - together with their own individual changes & vicissitudes.
>
> During the evening, Col. Boone went out & brought in a part of his buck, & Mrs. Boone soon prepared a warm & grateful pioneer supper. Having spent some days at Col. Boone's, Kenton & his son John, who was accompanying him, & about to depart - Simon took several fine blankets he & his son had on their horses, & gave them to Boone, together with a present of some money.

Simon Kenton Notes from John James, DM 5S 172. Members of the Boone family said that neither Daniel or Rebecca used tobacco in any form..

> I was much delighted with him - he was very conversable, very mild and pleasant and always willing to give any information...He was remarkable neat in his person and never wore hunting dress except when on hunting excursions.

Harriet M. Baber[?], granddaughter of Daniel Boone, DM 23C 34(2).

> Colo. Boone was one of the wonderful men of the world as much so as anyone celebrated in history, he possessed every virtue of humanity with[out]...any of the vices - always calm, self possessed and never thrown off his guard by passions[?]. He had an instinctive idea of courses & distances & could never be lost or be bewildered...in his greatest straights ...was never known to despair or give up to circumstances in all these respects his son Nathan late Colo of Dragoon USA[?] was ---- like him, he was always selected as pilot for every expedition that ever started[?] in the Country...

Stephen Hempstead, DM 16C 75(2) [capitalization and punctuation added].

> Col. Boone...explored new countries from the love of Nature...would tickle the soil with a hoe, and she would laugh you a bountiful harvest...where he could hunt and live at ease. He had no vague idea of empire, or rule, or profit. "I've opened the way for others to make fortunes but a fortune for myself was not what I was after."

Delinda Boone Craig, DM 30C 78.

> ...he took his cane at his bedside and... thumped on the coffin, & was satisfied it was all right...desired that it might be placed on a couple of chairs in the room.
>
> He said he would prefer to be shaved before dying; the negro Harry, who was in the habit of shaving him, now performed that office. Mrs. Callaway [Jemima Boone] was then requested to trim his hair, which she did... [Delinda] ...hoped he would live a long time... "No," said he quietly, "I am worn out."
>
> He had long been a great Bible reader. He said he had no fear of death - he had tried to do right. During the day, the 25th [Sept., 1820] he requested Mr. Craig [Delinda's husband] to preach his funeral sermon.
>
> ...Nearly sunrise, Sept. 26th, he desired that all his relatives should come in, that he might bid each good bye - saying he was going to a world of happiness, and he hoped they would not grieve at his departure... Having taken each by the hand, with a kind word, he then sent for the colored people, and bade them all a tender adieu... Then his son Nathan taking one of his hands ...and Mrs. Callaway...taking the other, he quietly breathed away his life, talking almost to the last moment - his last utterance being to his son: "I am going - don't foolishly grieve for me - my time has come". Now, when the sun was half an hour high, he breathed his last.

Delinda Boone Craig, DM 30C 81-3.

> ...I settled in St. Charles County [MO] in the fall of 1816, and from that time till his [Daniel Boone's] death, I was acquainted with Colo. Boon. He was a fine looking old man, of firm and manly stature, His mind possessed considerable native strength, without much of that polish, seldom attained in woods and uninhibited wildernesses. Much legendary stuff has been reported and published about this man, such as him and his wife making long trips by themselves up the Missouri, and returning with each a canoe loaded with furs and wild goose feathers. His capturing a wild savage man and bringing him down, who was only cloathed with long hair like a Bear &c. Colo. [Colonel] Boon died in his bed in then county of St. Charles and was intered on the farm of David Briant, now Warren County, and but a month or so ago the remains of him and his wife were disinterred, at the request of a committee from Kentucky, and carried to that state, with a view I suppose of paying due respect to his memory. Kentucky certainly owed this man a considerable debt of gratitude, and ought to have acknowledged it in his life time, but some more substantial benefit.

Benjamin Sharp, letter from Warren CO MO, 1845, DM 7C 25.

## REBECCA BRYAN BOONE

Mrs. Boone - She was a pattern of neatness in her dress and about her house. She said folks ought always to keep their things and horses in good order -that once tidings came that Col. Boone was very ill, & she was sent for to go to Richmond [Virginia] to attend him, & got ready and started in fifteen minutes. This was probably from Point Pleasant, at [the] mouth of the Kanhawa.
Delinda Boone Craig, daughter of Nathan Boone, interview, DM 30C 75.

Rebecca Bryan Boone - her hair was very black and so was her eyes. Her skin was not very fair. She was Rather a common sized woman. She was of a very mild and Pleasant speech and kind behaviour...
Daniel Bryan, DM 22C 19.

## SQUIRE BOONE

Recollects that his father said, that John Finley (rather advanced in years) came to the Yadkin settlements... praised up the Kentucky country - game plenty & buffalo - & so told Daniel & Squire Boone; & that he spoke[?] of the Falls of Ohio, how swift the water run[?], that the rapidity of the curent would take ducks & geese over the Falls & kill them - & that a person could go in a canoe below, & pick up as many of these fowls as he wanted. Thus would Finley work upon their feelings & relate adventures of the west, partly from a love of relating such things, & partly to secure their good services in taking care of his horse. This led the young men to think of the west, & thus introduced[?] an ardent desire to visit the country.
Moses Boone interview, DM 19C 1-2 [excerpts].

Squire Boone was 5 feet 10 inches - well made - sandy hair, light blue eye - blond? looks - always fond of hunting; not as much so as his brother Daniel: His wife survived him several years - died at her son Enoch Boone's...

[Squire Boone] said that when he first visited the Blue Licks, he saw numerous animals - herds of buffalo - panthers and wolves would catch for food the buffalo calves and deer - and lesser animals and vultures, buzzards, ravens, bald eagles & c, to eat the remains left by the wolf and the panthers. - 1770...
Moses Boone interview, DM 19C 47.

Squire Boone was born October 5th, 1744... died 5th August 1815 [September crossed out]. Jane VanCleve was born 16th October, 1749 in New Jersey...she and Squire Boone were married August 8th, 1765 [in the Yadkin country, North Carolina]. She died at her son, Enoch M. Boone's, at the mouth of Otter Creek, Ky, 10th March, 1829. Jonathan Boone, son of Squire and Jane Boone, was born 30th Aug., 1766...and died March, 1837 [January 1838 crossed out] Moses Boone was born Feb 23d, 1769...died 1852. Isaiah Boone was born March 13th, 1772... Sarah Boone was born Sept. 26th, 1774... married John Wilcox, and died in 1847... Enoch M. Boone was born Oct. 16th, 1777 at Boonesborough.

Enoch M. Boone, son of Squire Boone and Jane VanCleve, DM 19C 120.

Squire Boone - He said he was in 17 different fights and skirmishes - in '70 or '71 [1770 or 1771], when the Indians were killed - in '75 when Twitty was killed - in 3 affairs at Harrodsburg in '77 - Siege of Boonesborough in '78 - Clark's Campaign in '80; in Spring[?] of '81, when attacked near his fort, in Holder's defeat in '82 and on Clark's Campaign of '82 - others not recollected.

Squire Boone settled in Indiana in 1805. Was 5 feet 9 inches [tall], large muscles, strong arms, weighed about 160 pounds, black hair, sandy complexion, hazle eyes.

Enoch M. Boone, son of Squire, interview, DM 19C 153.

## ARABIA BROWN

Arabia Brown was an Indian spy for Daniel Boone. Was under Boone's command when they were making salt at Blue Licks [February 1778]...that shortly after he was taken prisoner, he got away from the Indians and returned to the Fort and was engaged in the most active and dangerous service for eight months...to go forth from the Fort looking out for Indians and Indian signs in order to give the alarm to the Fort in case of danger. That he was allowed one single pint of corn per day for 3 months of his service, and that he had to grind himself on a hand mill, that the balance of the time he had nothing furnished him but meat and that there was nothing else to give them. The reason why he served 8 months [instead of 6] was that he could not get back to Virginia until Squire Boone, a brother of Daniel Boone, was despatched with this affiant and others to Virginia to get more men. That he remained in Virginia some ten years after his return and then removed to Kentucky upwards of forty years ago [date not given] and has been living in the now County of Garrard long before it was a county.

Arabia (his mark) Brown

Arabia Brown's Deposition, DM 11C 44,44(1).

Arabia Brown was born in 1755 and entered service from Bedford Co Va in 1777. He died February 13, 1844 in Garrard Co KY.. He married in May, 1778 Elizabeth "Betsy" Dooley, who was a widow in Garrard Co KY, age 87 in 1844.

Pension statement from *Virginia/West Virginia Genealogical Data From Revolutionary War Pension and Bounty Land Warrant Records*, Vol. I (Wardell).

Obituary of Arabia Brown

*The Maysville Eagle*, Wednesday, March 27, 1844

Another Revolutionary Gone - Died at his residence in Garrard County, on Wednesday, the 13th instant, in the 89th year of his age, Mr. Arabia Brown, a soldier of the War of Independence, and one of the first settlers of Kentucky. He was a native of Virginia, but immigrated to this State at an early period, was engaged in a number of bloody skirmishes with the Indians, and was at the siege of Boonesborough. Throughout the whole period of his long career, he was

always marked for the industry of his habits, the kindness and liberality of his heart and the correctness with which he conducted his dealings with his fellow men. He was a member of the Presbyterian Church, and died in the hope of a glorious immortality beyond the grave. In a word, he was a soldier, a patriot, and a Christian. Rest in peace!
Shane Scrapbook of Newspaper Clippings, DM 29CC 12.

In 1818, Arabia Brown built a house in Lancaster, Kentucky (Garrard County) which is still standing.

## CLAIBORN BROWN

Claiborn Brown and his wife had both died before the pension acts were passed, but Harmon Brown, son of Claiborn Brown, gave a pension statement given in Clinton County, Kentucky in 1842. His father enlisted in Bedford County, Virginia under Col. Charles Watkins and joined Col. Boone, that Claiborn Brown served with John Brown and Richard Wade in Kentucky.

Richard Wade, also of Clinton County, Kentucky, declared that he had enlisted in Bedford County, Virginia for one year with John Brown, Claiborn Brown, Adam Brown, Ancel Goodman and others, about seventy men in all. After about six months, John Brown, Richard Wade, and Ancel Goodman were captured with Daniel Boone's saltmakers. Claiborn Brown was not captured but continued in service in the same neighborhood.

Barbary Luster, sister of Sarah Harmon who married Claiborn Brown, stated in 1839 (Wayne County, Kentucky) that she went with Sarah Harmon and Claiborn Brown to Newtondon [in Bedford County VA?] to Parson Holt's house when they were married. She did not remember the year they were married. [Abstracted from Dorman: *Virginia Revolutionary Pension Applications* 11:21.]

## WILLIAM BUCHANAN

Capt. William Buchanan - He was from Holston...had no family, don't recollect when he first came to Boonesborough, was killed in Holder's Defeat in 1782.
John Gass, DM 24C 75(4).

[Note: Holder's Defeat occurred in August, 1782 when John Holder hurriedly raised a company of men in an attempt to rescue two boys from near Boonesborough who had been captured by Indians. Jack Callaway and Jones Hoy from now Madison County, Kentucky were captured just before the siege at Bryan's Station and the Battle of Blue Licks. Holder's men encountered a greater number of Indians and were soundly defeated without recovering the boys, who were returned years later to their families.]

## FLANDERS CALLAWAY

...This was in the fall [1777?]. Some children sent outside of the fort to gather wood for an early breakfast ran back and said they had seen Indians in the fence corner - but they were discredited, as it was thought a ruse of get rid of gathering wood. The whites hurried to bring in the corn - and at breakfast time, a part went to breakfast and some remained to watch (Flanders Callaway and another person), and had set down there [sic] guns and shot pouches...and said to the sentinel, if there should be any alarm, to bring in the guns. While at breakfast, Indians fired on the sentinel, but missed. He fled, forgetting the guns - the balls knocking up the dirt all along. As he came in , Flanders Callaway [said], "where's my gun?"

"I never thought a word about it."

"But," said Callaway, "I am [in] a pretty fix - no gun - I must have my gun, even at the risk of my life, and I'll go for it."

The other man who had left his gun also [said] "if you go for yours, I will go for mine" - and resting a moment, they started back on full run...and were hotly fired on, balls whizzing all around them, and as they dashed through the gate, Callaway stubbed his toe against the bottom timber and fell - and the women exclaimed "Flanders Callaway is killed!" Jumping up, he replied, "I'm not hurt." The Indians fired the fort, but they were weak - and soon slipped away...
Susan Howell, daughter of Flanders and Jemima Boone Callaway, DM 23S 226.

He was a man of few words, and sterling worth.
Delinda Boone Craig interview, DM 30C 76.

## JEMIMA BOONE CALLAWAY

Jemima Callaway - medium sized - fine woman.
Abner Bryan [born 1802, son of Jonathan Bryan], DM 4C 51.

Jemima Boone...was a very brave and handsome girl...
Peter Houston, DM 20C 84(13).

## RICHARD CALLAWAY

Colo. Richard Callaway was born in Albemarle County, Virginia about the year 1729...He visited Kentucky before he removed his family there...with some 8 or 10 other men to examine the country ...camped out a great part of the trip coming out, had to graze their horses, as no provender could be obtained, and [they] frequently placed sentinels at night.
Richard P. Holder, descendant of John Holder, letter of October 1850 from Winchester, Tennessee, DM 24C 29.

Henderson's Ledger No. 52  Richard Callaway. A/c oped [account opened] Jan 6/76. Was killed, with Pemberton Rollins, on Canoe Ridge, about 2 miles from Boonsboro. He gotten an act from the Virginia legislature for the establishment of a ferry; and had cut down a tree, and was about to build a boat for a ferry. Capt. Hart lived in Col. Callaway's house, till he brought out his family in '79 [1779]. He was a fine, gallant man... Col. Callaway was from Bedford County, Virginia.

Richard Callaway was born about 1729 in Albemarle County, Virginia "a man of very firm appearance of about 150 pounds."
Letter of Richard P. Holder in 1850, grandson of John Holder, DM 24C 29(3).

From the Inhabitants of Boonesborough to George Rogers Clark
> Boonesborough, 10th March 1780

Sir...This day was Buried in one Grave the Late Colo. Richard Callaway and Lieutenant Pemberton Rawlings both of this Place...[they] were killed and scalped day before Yesterday almost in sight of Town...This...Tragical Scene we think portends very little good to that Settlement ...In this Critical and alarming situation we beg leave to implore your Assistance...

> Sir your most Humble Servts
> The Inhabitants of Boonesborough

As we have no regular officers to attest or certify the Publick doings of this Town, Capt. David Gass and Mr. John South are by unanimous consent Desired to sign their Names for and in behalf of the whole.

> David Gass
> John South

[Addressed:] Colo George Rogers Clark at the falls of the Ohio Favr Major Smith.
DM 50J 18-19.

Callaway killed - ... He was shot on Canoe Ridge about 2 miles from Boonesboro - when he ran some distance, and was tomahawked again...Capt. Hart's negroes...when they first saw him, took him for an indian, he was so bloody. From this place the negroes took him into the Fort.
Nathaniel Hart, DM 17CC 193.

## FLANDERS CALLAWAY

[Before 1809] Flanders Callaway & wife rode on horseback to Kentucky all the way from Missouri - & visited friends & relatives there.

Flanders Callaway was a tall, spare, thin-visaged, swarthy man.
John Scholl, DM 22S 271.

Grandfather [Flanders] Callaway was a small, hearty, trim-built man, dark complexion, keen black eye - rather a pixey[?] old man is my recollection of him... he or grandmother never drew any Pention.
Evisa L. Coshow, letter, Jan 24 1886, DM 21C 58(1).

## JACK CALLAWAY

Age 3 at the time of the siege, Jack Callaway had already lived during the capture of two of his sisters from Fort Boonesborough in 1776, and would lose his father, Col. Richard Callaway, to the Indians' tomahawk in 1780. He himself was captured in 1782 and held captive for about two years. See "What Shall I Do Now? The Indian Captivities of Margaret Paulee, Jones Hoy and Jack Callaway 1779- ca 1789," *Filson Club History Quarterly*, 70: 363-404, October 1996 (edited by Anne Crabb).

Moses Boone escorted Jack back to Boonesborough when he returned from captivity [1784] and later told Draper about it: "Jack could talk English, but quite an Indian - settled in Shelby County, and became a very respectable and prominent man." Robert Hancock in 1853 to Lyman Draper (DM 24C 22) describes the adult John Callaway: "six feet tall, dark complexion, dark, penetrating eyes".

John Callaway was about six feet high, well built, inclined to be fleshy, settled in Henry County Kentucky and in 1813 commanded a ridgment [regiment] under Govnor Shelby and joined General Harrison and was with him at the battle of Thames and a few years after died in Henry County. They [Jones Hoy and Jack Callaway] both lived and died respected.
Samuel Boone to Lyman Draper, 1854, DM 22C 72(5).

## KESIAH CALLAWAY - See Dolly

## AMBROSE COFFEE

I was born in the city of Dublin in Ireland and from the best accounts that I have received of my parents, I was between 12 and 13 years of age when I came to America.
Deposition of Ambrose Coffee in 1809, Madison County, KY Deed Book Letter I, pp. 92ff. (Land Suit of Henry Banta)

Deposeth: that in the year Eighty [1780] he was at this place in company with Col. Richard Callaway...then I and Callaway returned from this place to Boons borough and some time in the said year Eighty myself and Pembleton [Pemberton] Rollins came Hunting in these woods, and happened to come by the Spring and camped all night and Rollins asked me if I Noad [knowed] who claimed this place. my answer to him was that I was informed by Colo Richard Callaway that it belonged to Ben Harrison. the place was very much taken with cain [cane]... in the morning we went to get our horses...and so went from this place to Boons Borough...
Ambrose Coffee's Deposition for Ben Harrison. Clark County, Kentucky Depositions, Kentucky State Archives Microfilm Reel #259295, p. 378

## JESSE CONWAY

Jesse Conway gave his pension statement in Madison County, Illinois in 1832 when he was age 71. He stated that he enlisted in 1777 with Capt. William Buchanan, Lt. Joseph Drake and Ensign Ephraim Drake at Reed Island in Virginia. In June, 1777, they marched under Col. Bowman to Boonesborough where he was under Col. Daniel Boone and remained in service for eighteen months. He was discharged soon after the siege of Boonesborough and returned home to Reed Island.

The following year he returned to Kentucky under Capt. Isaac Riddle [Ruddell] and was stationed on Licking River. On June 24, 1780, he was captured when Capt. Bird's army attacked the stations on Licking River: Ruddell's and Martin's. A large number of prisoners were marched to Detroit; he was confined until 1784. Jesse Conway was married to Margaret Renfro when he died in 1840.
*Virginia Revolutionary Pensions* 22: 27-8, (Dorman)

## JOHN CONWAY

John Conway was age 75 on August 10th...enlisted in 1776 to guard the lead mines for six months... In May 1777, he enlisted for eighteen months under Capt. William Buchanan and Col. John Bowman, marched to Boonesborough, Kentucky, where he served out his eighteen months guarding the fort, was there during the siege and Col. Boone was one of the commanders.

He remained in Kentucky after his discharge and in April, 1779 he lived at Capt. Isaac Riddle's station on south fork of Licking River and served as guard and Indian spy until June 24, 1780 when the fort was attacked and many were captured by Indians under Capt. Bird. He was marched to Detroit with the other prisoners and kept there until 1784 when he was liberated and returned to Kentucky.

He served in Col. Benjamin Logan's campaign against the Piqua Town of Indians...defeated them and took prisoners... He lost his discharges when captured as the Indians robbed him of everything.

He was born in Henrico County, Virginia on August 10, 1758 and has a record in his Bible. He was living in Montgomery County, Virginia when he entered service. He has lived in Kentucky the whole time since the Revolutionary War except the time he was prisoner.

Robert McDaniel and Ann Mary Spears told that they were living at Ruddle's Station when it was attacked, that they were captured by the Indians with John Conway and taken to Detroit...
Abstract of a Pension Statement given on February 13, 1834, Nicholas County, Kentucky. *Virginia Revolutionary Pension Applications*, vol. 22: 28-30, (Dorman).

John Conway, entered service in 1776 from Montgomery Co VA. He was born Aug. 10, 1758 in Henrico CO VA, applied for pension in 1834 in Nicholas Co KY, and died June 15, 1837. He married Anna Sutton, of Bourbon Co., KY in April 1790. She was born June 24, 1766, applied for widow's pension in 1843 in Nicholas Co., KY, and was still living there in 1848.
*Virginia/West Virginia Revolutionary War Pension and Bounty Land Warrant Records*, Vol. I (Wardell).

## WILLIAM CRADLEBAUGH

Cradlebaugh ..skilled in woodcraft... of remarkable endurance, bravery and acumen as a scout...hunter and trapper, unpretentious towards everything... He was wedded to his flintlock gun and scalping knife and very much attached to his dog. With this equipment he could feed his family and the inhabitants of the forts with deer, buffalo, elk, etc., which abounded.
Henderson's Ledger, DM 17CC [punctuation added].

William Cradlebaugh - born 1744 North Carolina, died 1833 Madison Co KY. Went to Boonesborough in 1776 and was there through the troubles of 1777-1778. Served in Bowman's Campaign 1779, Clark's in 1780, Logan's in 1786 - was express to Kanhawa, swimming creeks and rivers and procuring his food that way. Settled near Boonesborough in Madison County, Kentucky, received a pension and died in 1833 age 88.
DM 4B 123(1) note 1.

William Cradlebaugh - Madison County, Kentucky - Declaration August 30, 1832 - aged 88 years. That he came from North Carolina to Kentucky in 1776, & settled at Boonesborough - was then enlisted to do fort duty & act as guard & Indian spy till May, 1779, which there was a company raised by Col. Bowman to go to the Chillicothe towns: We there attacked the indians & followed them in their retreat half way into the town, when we were ordered to proceed no further: Several Indians were killed, among them was the chief Black Fish. That he served in another expedition, in 1780, under Ben. Logan & George Rogers Clark was the commander as ------ went beyond the Chillicothe towns the name of the place does not recollect; but 12 or 13 Indians were killed: He served another expedition under Daniel Boone & Col. Thos. Kennedy, upon which he proceeded almost as far as the head of Mad River: on this expedition (Logan's 1786) were killed 12 or 13 warriors, & took 32 prisoners, & destroyed 3 towns. He was at three sieges of Boonesboro: He once went as an express from Kentucky to Kenhawa, started without provisions & swam the rivers & creeks, a distance of 200 miles; That he served at different times[?] under Capt. Daniel Boone, Capt. John Holder, & Col.[?] Callaway, who commanded the Fort at Boonesboro subsequently to Capt Boone or after he was promoted. Was living 27th April 1833.

Declaration of William Cradlebaugh, DM 1 OO 65.

Deposition of William Cradlebaugh [in the suit Bedinger vs. Walker Heirs, Madison County, Ky Circuit Court], 9th of June, 1815. He was paid $1.00 for 2 days' attendance.

Question: you recollect the most of us raising corn at Bushes Settlement near Boonsborough in the summer 1779?
Answer: I cannot recollect it for I was mutch from home. ...I went into North Carolina in the year 1787 or 1788 and Staid there four or five years and returned back again to Kentucky and settled at Warens[?] Station and lived there about three years and then moved to where I now live.

The Bedinger Papers, DM 1A 166.

William Cradlebaugh. Was in Boone's Fort...Was at Estill Station. Veteran Indian fighter and hunter. In General Clark's raid on the Miami towns. When Pickaway [Piqua, Ohio] was captured [Cradlebaugh] found three balls of sugar weighing a pound each. Thought he would eat two and carry the third home, but found it so good he ate all three. "As good as Cradlebaugh's sugar" became a saying. Would not have but 60 acres of land. Had three children. The house in which he lived, after quitting fort life, still stands near Richmond... One of only 3 or 4 who were not wounded [at the Battle of Little Mountain, also called Estill's Defeat, 1782]. His walking-cane, made while resident of Boonesborough, is preserved by his descendants...
[His] house still standing in ruins, built about 1790, or earlier. Puncheons yet good. Small white-oak logs - 6 or 8 inches in diameter. Boards put on with pins...

From French Tipton Papers, Memorandum Book I: 34. [No source is listed for this information.]

William Cradlebough - wife was Sybel Moore, sister to Nathan Moore who was killed by Indians, was an important all-around man at the fort at Boonesborough...descendants now living in Estill County, KY.. His name should appear on the Monument...

He lies buried on the south side of the Speedwell Pike [Madison County, KY]...with only rough stones put at the head and foot.

Some of their children were:

Didamah Cradlebaugh- married Hawkins Harris, son of Tyree Harris and wife, Miss Gooch.

Elizabeth Cradlebaugh - married Isaac May

Susan Cradlebaugh - married Caleb Todd

William H.. Miller Unpublished Manuscript, (microfilm), Vol. I, article #244 "Cradlebaugh."

William Cradlebaugh besides owning a claim to a body of very fertile land in Bourbon County, owned some good land on the headwaters of Otter Creek in Madison County, KY, just a mile or so south east of Richmond, upon which he settled, lived and died.

At the time being much litigation over land claims and titles in Kentucky, to avoid suits at law, William Cradlebaugh disposed of his Bourbon County Lands claim for a gun, and was very proud of his trade, as his claim might prove unavailable, and the gun was the friend upon which he ever relied - with his unerring aim - for the protection of himself and family from assaults of the Indians, and also with it he procured game...

He lived near to Estill's Station, and on an occasion when out scouting, he was cut off from his approach to his cabin by Indians on his trail, and it was for more than a day he could not enter his cabin, and he necessarily became very hungry, and at a point on Muddy Creek near the ford at the present little hamlet of Colyer, and close to the spot where David G. Martin, Jr., at a much later date built a house and lived (now owned by Reuben Cox). William Cradlebaugh killed a buffalo, and cutting choice pieces from the hams, retired to a nearby sinkhole on the hill, and in the sinkhole cooked and ate and camped till the next day, when he stealthily crept from his hiding place through the brush to his cabin, and joyfully found his wife and children had escaped injury by the hands of the savages and were all right.

Harris Family File, Eastern Kentucky University Library, Special Collections and Archives.

## ISADORE CHENE

He died... about a year of two after the war of 1812-1814... He was a good kind of man - rigid with the Indians as British agent - a good sized man, nearly six feet, and heavy form.

Peter Navarre, born 1788 in Detroit, DM 17S 136.

He was long an Indian interpreter for the British Indian department - took part in councils, regarded by the Indians as a great leader. Died when he was about 80.

Mrs. Rosalie Chabert Larouge', DM 17S 189.

Isidore Chene died June 29, 1793, aged 56 years.

St. Anne's Catholic Church Register, DM 17S 188.

## DOLLY

The following was written after the 1840 Boonesborough Celebration of the settlement of Kentucky.

...People from all parts of Kentucky and beyond, began to arrive. Saturday, 24th, ceremonies began at II o'clock and simultaneously one of the hardest rains ever known to have fallen...Gen. Smith [went] across in the boat to meet Mrs. French [Kesiah Callaway]... Mrs. French's servant, who was in the fort, John Hart, and other pioneers present.

Flanagan [not explained] says: Mrs. French had Dolly with her - servant in Fort. "Why do you cry?" "It makes me think of the time the British and Indians came to take us".

French Tipton Papers Memorandum Book II: 262. Article on the Boonesborough Celebration, Saturday, May 23, 1840.

There was not a dry eye to be seen. Mrs. French [Kesiah Callaway] was received in dignified silence. The servant Dolly was placed next to Mrs. French by John Hart, another veteran of the siege...

Newspaper account in the *Farmer's Chronicle*, William L. Neale, editor, from an original paper belonging to Judge W. R. Shackelford, Richmond, KY, June 6, 1840 in *Register of the Kentucky Historical Society*: 24, 1926, pp. 175-181.

## PIERRE DROUILLARD
[This name was spelled "Drewyer" by some of the Americans.]

A pioneer, Joseph Wade, reported "Drewyer's" visits to Kenton:

Drewyer often visited Kenton...often saw and talked with him - talked pretty good English...bragging about his fame & wealth: Was small in size, & lived much with Kenton - who gave him a horse to ride backwards & forwards between Kenton & the Indian towns.

Pierre Drouillard and brothers Simon, Joseph, Francis, lived on the British side of the Detroit river. Pierre was an Indian trader with the Shawnees. Rather tall, slim, and swarthy...He was Indian interpreter and commissary in the Indian Department, distributing Indian goods from the Government store at Detroit. He died April 14, 1803, age about 60.

Robert F. Navarre, DM 17S 157, 185, 188.

Pierre Drouillard was born in Detroit, was long a trader with the Shawanoe Indians. Had a son George by a Shawanoe woman - afterwards married Angeline Labade[?], had two daughters and a son...He was long [a] British Indian interpreter and commissary in the Indian Department - distributing Indian goods from the Government store at Detroit. He went off, was gone a good many years (visited New York in 1786 - LCD), don't know where - when he returned he was not in British service. He died in Detroit in 1804. Appeared old, sixty to seventy - over six feet [tall], rawboned - thoroughly acquainted with Indian languages.

Mrs. Pelage Drouillard, born 1786, daughter-in-law of Peter Drouillard, and her son Frances H. Drouillard near Windsor, Canada, DM 17S 185.

Pierre Drouillard died April 14, 1803 aged about 60 years.

St. Anne's Catholic Church Register, DM 17S 188.

## DAVID GASS

David Gass was born in 1732 in Pennsylvania, was living in Albemarle County, Virginia where he served in the militia; he was Lieutenant in Washington County, Virginia. He came to Kentucky with Daniel Boone 1774 and 1775, lived in Fort Boonesborough with his family three years, then moved to Estill Station in 1781 and lived five years. Capt. Gass was in Col. John Bowman's Company in 1781. [This does not account for the years 1779-1781.]

In 1784 he began to improve what afterwards was his home and the first county seat of Madison County, KY, "Milford". The county formed in 1785, and in 1786 the second session of county court met in Capt. David Gass's house and continued meeting there until a court house was built. He was appointed by Patrick Henry, Governor of Virginia, as Judge of the Court of Quarter Sessions which was organized in his house and held its sessions there till the first Courthouse was built at Milford. This famous "Quarter Session Court" was the highest tribunal west of Williamsburg.

David Gass had land grants in Madison, Bourbon, Fayette, and Lincoln Counties, Kentucky. He lived on his own land which lies on both sides of [now] Lancaster Road and near about the unforgotten burg which he established with others [Milford?]. David Gass died testate in Madison County in 1806 and was buried in the grave yard which he selected and which a deed in Madison County Courthouse is recorded of ¼ acre forever to be held. Vandals have taken the stones away, and since plowed over the graves. This is located near the village of Caleast on the Lancaster Road [western Madison County, KY].

His daughters were the belles of Milford. Mary and Sarah married sons of James Black, Sr., Revolutionary Soldier. Sarah Gass Black died in 1831 at the age of 95. She was proud of her record, moulding bullets and getting water [at the Siege of Boonesborough in 1778] and told this to her grand daughter Jane Black, then 15 years old. She was buried in the Black Cemetery near Lancaster Road in Madison County, Kentucky. The grave is marked.

Turley Noland Papers: Revolutionary Soldiers of Madison County, KY [two versions from this source are compiled here].
The Turley Noland Papers are held by Special Collections and Archives, Eastern Kentucky University Library. Sources cited by Mrs. Noland: Wisconsin Historical Society, Family Bibles, Court Records.

...I, David Gass...of Madison County Kentucky, for love, goodwill, and affection which I have and bear toward my loving son John Gass of the county of Bourbon...550 acres...that I...hold by Patent, bearing date July the fifth, 1784...in Bourbon County on Stoner's Creek...below Nathaniel Randall's spring...with appurtenances...as a Deed of Gift...in the year...1798...

Signed: David Gass

Witnesses: William Gass, James Gass, John Mitchell
Bourbon County KY Deed Book E: 21.

## JOHN GASS [Son of David Gass.]

In '76 [1776], in February when John Gass first went there, there was no such thing as stockading then or when he left in the fall. [Apparently David Gass and son John visited Boonesborough in 1776 before returning to Virginia to escort the rest of the family to Kentucky.]

Boone & Callaway had cabins...below the lick & near where the ferry now is and there may have been another cabin or so there for Callaway's negroes...

Col. [Richard] Henderson, Samuel Henderson, John Floyd and others claimed[?] together, lived above Boone & Callaway some 300 yards. Neither place was stockaded in '76...

[After Indian troubles] they all concentrated at Henderson's, built stockades...Boone's & Callaway's places were burnt...

Draper's interview with John Gass in 1844, DM 24C 74(8).

I had a sister [Jennie] killed at Estill's Station. It was March [1782]. That night the snow had fallen. The sugar orchard was on the north west side from the Station. This was after Capt. James Estill's negro was taken. Sam Estill's negro Monk had gone out with my sister, she to see if the trees were dripping (the sugar water was running), he to a spring that was out there to haul some wood on the --- ----. They saw the Indians first and made for the Station. My sister got within 20[?] yards of the fort, and could have ----- but then came across from the other side of the fort... and they shot her...

Shane Interview with John Gass, DM 11CC 15.

I, John Gass of the County of Bourbon and State of Kentucky, do make my last Will and Testament in manner and form following...

First...my son David Gass shall have the lot of ground where on my son James Gass lived...

Second. Mitchell Gass [son] is to have the...ground he lives on...up Samuel Clay's line...to a water gap on Stoner below the Big Spring...

Third...Betsy Alexander is to receive $2000 if she outlives her present husband John Alexander...if she dies first the $2000 is to be equally divided between the children of David Gass, Mitchell M. Gass and Polly Brooks.

Fourth...I bequeath to the [underage] children of my daughter Polly Brooks one hundred acres of land..

Fifth. It is my will that the residue of my land not otherwise disposed of shall be sold and that $2000 of the proceeds shall be appropriated by my executors in the sending my negroes to Liberia, that is to say in clothing and all other materials such as tools, cooking materials, keeping them six months after they are there as well as expenses of transportation, and if that sum is not sufficient for all of those purposes as much more as will be sufficient shall be taken from the sale money of said land.

Sixth. The negroes to be sent to Liberia are named as follows: Phebe and her two sons Jack and Jake; Amanuel and Austin; Esther and her four children Harriet, Cube, Ann, and Nancy; Angeline and her daughter[s?] Lieu, Sarah and Charity; Lucinda and her three children York, Delphia and Silas and all others she may have.

Seventh. It is my will that such of those negroes as shall refuse to go to Liberia shall be sold to go down the River and the money for which they are sold shall be given to those who do go.

Eighth. It is my will [that] the children of my late daughter Jane, namely James and John Alexander and Ann Roseman shall have $200 each...

Ninth...specie money in the hands of Mitchell M. Gass shall remain in his hands until a substantial stone wall shall be built around my graveyard including one fourth of an acre...

Tenth...my cash notes and personal estate of every description not otherwise disposed of shall be equal right of all the children of my sons David Gass, Mitchell M. Gass and my late daughter Polly Brooks...4th day July 1854.

John Gass (Seal)

Abstract from Bourbon County KY Wills.

John Gass died on Dec. 24, 1855 and his will was proved in 1856 in Bourbon County, Kentucky.

## JOHN GASS [nephew of David Gass]

My cousin John Gass... 15 or 20 years older than [himself]...
John Gass letter, 1848, DM 24C 91.

In July, 1776 Indians captured Jemima Boone, Betsy and Fanny Callaway from Fort Boonesborough. The girls had been out in the boat and when they were captured, the boat remained on the opposite side of the Kentucky River, preventing the rescue party from following them.

[Daniel] Boone, [John] Floyd, David Gass & his nephew John Gass ...William Bush, John McMillen, & Samuel Henderson, were of the pursuing party...& John Gass swam over for the boat, a venture much applauded at the time.
John Gass, DM 24C 74(9).

## ELIZABETH GENTRY

...Miss Elizabeth Gentry, wife of Mr. Bowman. Miss Elizabeth Gentry was in the fort at Boonesborough during the stormy period... knew Daniel Boone, Squire Boone, and their wives, Simon Kenton, Flanders Callaway, Thomas Brooks, Jesse Copher and others...was in the fort when the girls were captured...She also said she moulded bullets for the defenders of the fort - more especially when besieged by Indians, often with whites siding [with] them [the British fought with the Indians] - Simon Girty, the renegade, was there with them once, and she would bite the necks of the bullets with her teeth till her lips would get too sore to do so.
John H. Brandenburgh, informant, of Madison County, Kentucky. William H. Miller Unpublished Manuscript, Vol. I, article #180a (no page number). [This is the only mention of Miss Elizabeth Gentry's having been present during the Siege of Boonesborough and before.]

## WILLIAM AND STEPHEN HANCOCK

My father [Stephen Hancock] was born in the year 1736 - died 1824 (88 years old). My uncle [William Hancock] was born 1738 - died 1821 (83 years old). He was too old in the war of 1812. He has no children to my knowledge - last I heard from him he had but one son & I think he is dead.

My father & uncle did both live in Madison County, Ky...my Father was about 5 feet 8 inches [?] high, about 160 pounds each. They were both nearer alike in every respect than most any other two men. My father a little bowlegged - my uncle straight as an indian.

They were both there - in Blue Lick battle...My father had one bullet shot through his hat, one through his shirt sleeve.

Robert Hancock, son of Stephen, letter of 1853, DM 24C 22(1), 22(2), 22(3).

William Hancock was born in Goochland County, Virginia, in 1738 and served on Col. Byrd's Cherokee Expedition near the close of the old French and Indian War & first visited Kentucky in 1775. Returning[?] to Virginia in the fall of that year, he removed to Boonesborough early in 1777, & took part in the contests there that season with the Indians. Escaping from his captivity, he shared in the long siege of Boonesboro, in September 1778, & served in Clark's Campaigns of 1780 & 1782, and in the battle of Blue Licks. After the Indians wars he settled on a farm in Madison County, Kentucky till 1797, when he removed to Missouri[?] and died in St. Charles County in that state in 1828, in the 83rd year of his age. He was a man of medium height, about five feet 8 inches, straight as an Indian, & for many years was an Exemplary member of the Baptist denomination.

Lyman Draper's footnote from his compilation, DM 4B 196-7.

## JOHN HART - See also Dolly

After Nathaniel Hart was killed by Indians, his son John went to Maryland to live with his uncle Thomas Hart for several years.

From Mrs. Mary Irvine Hart, daughter of Lydia Callaway and husband Christopher Irvine, granddaughter of Col. Richard Callaway. Mary Irvine Hart married John Hart (1773-1846), son of Nathaniel Hart, DM 18S 211-214.

## SAMUEL HENDERSON

When the news of the girls' captivity came to the knowledge of [Samuel] Henderson (the affianced of Elizabeth Callaway, one of the captives) he was engaged in shaving himself, laid aside his razor & went off with the other half shaved - & was much joked in consequence, in connection with his known engagement to Miss Callaway.

John Gass, DM 24C 75(2).

While at Boonesborough, I had the pleasure of being present at the first wedding that took place in Kentucky. A man by the name of Sam Henderson was married to Betsy Callaway. Daniel Boone officiated as minister [others say Squire Boone, Daniel's brother, officiated] and celebrated the rights [sic] of matrimony. The dress of the bride and groom would not, at this day, be thought altogether Suited for Such an occasion. Henderson's hunting shirt having been threadbare by time and rough usage, he borrowed mine in which he was married.

Nathan Reid, DM 10NN 109.

[In his Life of Boone in volume 4B, Lyman Draper gave the date for the wedding as August 7, 1776.]

Samuel Henderson, whose father bore the same name, was born in Granville County, North Carolina, February 6th, 1746. He accompanied his brother, Col. Richard Henderson, to Watauga, early in 1775, and was present at the treaty. He formed one of Henderson's party that followed Boone's trail to Kentucky... He aided in the defence of Boonesborough during the attacks on that place in 1777 and 1778, and next year went with his family on a visit to North Carolina...

[Samuel Henderson] held the office of Colonel of the Militia of his county in North Carolina. In 1807, he removed to Tennessee, first locating in Hawkins, and then, in 1811, migrating to Franklin County. Aside from the offices indicated and that of a Magistrate, he was not engaged in public life, preferring to spend his days as independent cultivator of the soil. His death occurred in Warren County, Tennessee, Dec. 16th, 1816, at about the age of sixty-five years. He had blue eyes, was six feet in height, well proportioned, possessing great muscular powers, weighing about two hundred pounds; fearless, kind, affectionate and humane.
Lyman Draper's Notes, DM 5B 77-8.

## JESSE HODGES

Madison County, Kentucky - Declaration 4th Sept. 1832, aged 72 years in November next. That he entered the service in July 1777 in Bedford County, Virginia for 18 months - was a native of & then resided in Goochland County, but enlisted in Bedford. His captain was Charles G. Watkins, & his company was in what he understands was the Virginia State troops. He enlisted to come to Kentucky to defend the country: John Milam was Lieutenant, & David Carns [probably Crews], Ensign. We were immediately marched to Boonesboro, where we continued to do duty as soldiers, guarding the fort, spying for Indians & hunting for meat for the people in the fort. He was there during the great siege of 1778, of 11 days, by 300 or 400 Indians. That he continued at Boonesborough after his 18 months service was out, & did duty as spy until the end of the war. In May 1779, he went on Col. Bowman's campaign across the Ohio against the Indians in Capt. John Holder's company - went to the Pickaway towns (in 1780) - was in the battle - burnt the cornfields - Gen. George Rogers Clark commanded. He also served as a volunteer on Clark's campaign of 1782...
Pension Application of Jesse Hodges, DM 1 OO 62, part I.

Hodges was born in Goochland County, Virginia in November, 1760, and came to Kentucky in Capt. Watkins' [or Gwatkins'] Company in the fall of 1777. He was in the big Siege of Boonesborough in 1778, and served on Bowman's Expedition in 1779, and on Clark's of 1780 and 1782, and was for many years engaged in the defence of the country. He enjoyed a pension and died in Madison County, Kentucky in 1838, leaving behind him the fragrance of a good name.
Excerpts from Draper's comments, DM 4B 127(1) note 2.

1808 - I came to Boonesborough in October 1777 and lived there until 1785 and have lived within 3 miles thereof ever since... I know of one place called Boonesborough in the world.

Deposition of Jesse Hodges in the suit Banta heirs versus Green Clay, Madison County, KY Circuit Court Records: Complete Record Book B: 328.

## JOHN HOLDER

Mrs. French [Keziah Callaway, sister-in-law of John Holder] has informed me that Col. Holder was a man of rather uncommonly commanding appearance - great energy of character.
R. G. Williams[?] letter of 1861, DM 24C 43.

John Holder had a Captain's Commission from Virginia and commanded at Boonesboro. Came from near Winchester[?] Frederick County, Virginia. Came to Boonesboro, married Fanny Callaway - a daughter of Col. Callaway, who had several daughters...Some of Holder's sons live near Boonesborough... He was a large 6 foot man - not brilliant[?] - but useful. Dark complexion.
The Bedinger Papers, DM 1A 69.

My grandfather and grandmother [Fanny Callaway and John Holder] were married something like a year after [the siege]...yet they were engaged at the time of the siege. Both marriages [that of his grandparents and Betsy Callaway and Samuel Henderson] took place in vicinity of Boonesborough...

He done a good deal of fighting against the Indians was afterwards a magistrate and was a private a Captain and a Colo in Revolutionary War. He lived to be 62 years old...height was about ordinary, weighed generally 160 to 170 was a man of very firm appearance said to be when in his prime very handsome and a man of a good deal more than ordinary agility and strength...
Letter of Richard P. Holder in 1850, grandson of John Holder, DM 24C 29(4).

Maj. John Holder - he was a young man between 22 and 25 years old. came from Virginia to North Carolina to see his friends at the time and place where Capt. William Bailey Smith was Raising his Volunteer Company to March to Kentucky. Then and there Holder joined the company, he was a fine looking young man, full six feet high, of a fair complexion, grey Eyes &c. After the company randivond [rendezvoued?], Holder was chosen Lieutenant as was the other under officers - all chosen by the company[?]. Holder married a Daughter of Colo. Richard Callaway.
Letter of Daniel Bryan, 1843, when he was age 86, DM 22C 9(10) (14 marked out).

[John Holder probably lived for a time on the north side of Kentucky River in Clark County, near the site of present-day Hall's Restaurant. Apparently he operated a commissary there.]

Mr. Reuben Proctor in account with John Holder
To 1 quart of whiskey July 1784..................0.4.0
To 1[?] Bushel of Corn July 1784...............0.5.0
To 1 quart of whiskey..................................0.2.6
To 1 quart of whiskey..................................0.2.6

    To 4 Gallons & a half of whiskey ............... 1.7.0
    For[?] Buck skins a 6/pr Skin .................... 0.12.0
    as per Note given to Anthony -------
        Hundley Decr 25$^{th}$ 1786 ...................... 2.13.0

Madison County Kentucky Court of Quarter Sessions, Circuit Court Case Files, Box 11. Holder v. Arthur.

## HORN

Aaron Horn, Sr., died soon after the siege. Family tradition has it that he was wounded while working in the field with a machete soon after the siege was over and died from this wound. He left a widow Elizabeth, three underage sons, and no will. In 1779, Elizabeth Horn obtained a pre-emption certificate for 400 acres. She made an agreement with James Estill to "locate and clear out...400 acres of land for her...and [he] took his obligation to convey to her 200 acres thereof when a grant should be obtained". The eldest Horn son, Christopher, then came to Kentucky to claim his father's land. Aaron Horn Sr.'s widow and sons were living on the land in question, and after several years of threats from the eldest son to take the land from his mother, a suit was filed in Madison County, KY Circuit Court in 1802 between Elizabeth Horn and eldest son Christopher Horn.

The land lies in today's Estill County, Kentucky above Coperas Lick, between Cow Creek and Millers Creek. The court transcript states that Aaron and Elizabeth Horn and their sons came to Kentucky "in the year 1778...and very shortly thereafter her husband departed this life". Depositions taken in 1802-1803 state that Aaron Horn died in late September or early October, 1778. In 1779, Elizabeth Horn hired out her sons William, Mathias, and Aaron Jr., to grow corn "on the halves" with Thomas Deal. William and Mathias gave depositions that all three of the brothers were underage in 1779. Mathias said in his deposition: "The old woman frequently came to me and cried and told me of his [Christopher Horn's] threats [to take the land] and said if he sued her it would take all she had left (the Indians having taken all their horses and part of their cattle)..."

Joseph Proctor gave a deposition stating he had heard Christopher Horn threaten his mother. He said: "The old woman appeared very uneasy about it. She being not able to read or write in English."

In 1832 Mathias Horn was age 70 and living in Estill County, Kentucky. He enlisted on Holston River in Virginia and came to Kentucky under Captain Riddle, arriving at Fort Boonesborough in April 1778. During 1778 and part of 1779, he was under Capt. Benjamin Logan and continued as a soldier and Indian spy until 1779, when he went with Capt Logan and George Rogers Clark in a campaign against the Indians. He continued at Fort Boonesborough, was there in the Great Siege in 1778, and went on a campaign against the Indians in 1780, and continued as a soldier at Boonesborough until the close of the Revolutionary War except when out on campaigns or when ordered out as Indian spy or ranger. In 1839, Susanna Horn, age 77, widow of Mathias, appeared in court and said she married Mathias Horn in the summer of 1782 in Fayette County, Kentucky [at Boone's Station, according to Joseph Proctor's statement]. Mathias Horn died in January, 1834.

Joseph Proctor age 84 in 1839, said he lived with Horn's father, and enlisted with Mathias Horn, knew him from the year 1776, and married his sister in 1777. Polly Proctor, age 80 in 1839, stated that she lived two miles from Boone's Station when the Horns were there.

Aaron Horn [Jr], aged 77 in 1839, at his own house in Madison County, Kentucky, stated that he was present at the wedding of Mathias and Susan Horn.

William Horn, age 74 in July, 1839, stated that he was present at the wedding of the above.

Madison County KY Circuit Court Case for June Term 1803 transcribed by Edward Puckett; copies provided by Kathleen Noland Calder. Family data also provided by Diana Frymyer. Pension Statement of Mathias Horn abstracted from *Estill County [KY] and Its People* II:78-79 (Estill County Historical and Genealogical Society, Ravenna KY 1988, submitted by Wayne and Ruth Horn).

## MOLUNTHA

Moluntha was the brother-in-law of Shawnee Chief Cornstalk who was murdered in 1777. He had been with Duquesne at the Siege of Boonesborough and accused Boone there of killing his son, which Boone denied. He was also at the Battle of Blue Licks. While Moluntha was a prisoner carrying a white flag, Hugh McGary killed him with an axe, for which McGary was court-martialed at Bardstown [KY] on March 2, 1787, and found guilty.

*Bryant's Station*, Reuben L. Durrett, Louisville: John P. Morton & Co., 1897, Filson Club Publication, No. 12: 111n.

## EDWARD AND MARGARET NELSON

His grandfather, Edward Nelson, was a native of Culpepper County, Virginia - early went to Yadkin, Rowan County, North Carolina, where he was mostly raised - migrated to Boonesborough with his family (my informant's father [probably John] two years old - born in 1773, and died in 1858, at age of 85 - must have gone in 1775 to Boonesborough - was there when the Boone and Callaway girls were taken - and during the long siege. LCD).

Mrs. Edward Nelson said she had made salt from the water from the sulphur well at Boonesborough - very tedious -it taking 60 gallons for a pound [of salt]... Mrs. Nelson died in 1839. [Probably in Clark County, KY.]

William Nelson, age 60, grandson of Edward Nelson, interviewed by Draper near Boonesborough, Kentucky [date given at end of interview: Sept. 8th & 9th, 1863], DM 18S 230-232.

...at the time said agreement was made between her husband and [James] Estill, it was also agreed between them that they would draw writings the next day: & it was put off from time to time...she heard her husband say, not more than two months before his death that he never had transferred the said certificate granted by the [Land] Commissioners to James Estill.

[signed] Margarett Nelson

Accompanying the depositions is a patent dated 1788 (survey date 1783) for the land in contention in 1810. A plat shows Nelson's 1000 acres on Strode's Fork in what was then Fayette County, Kentucky, probably today's Bourbon County. The land abutted James Estill's and Green Clay's lines. The "markers and director" of the survey were John Gass, William Estill, and David Gass. Green Clay signed the survey as Deputy Surveyor [of Madison County, Kentucky].

From Green Clay Papers, University of Kentucky Archives: Depositions taken 25th January 1810 (in a suit of Nelson's Heirs vs. Estill's heirs). The deposition of Margarett Nelson, widow of Edward Nelson.

Children of Edward and Margaret Nelson were:
John, born in 1773, married Dicy, died in Fayette County, KY 1858.
William, married Dulcenia Crews 29 Jun 1797 in Madison County, KY, died 1811-1818.
Moses
Elizabeth, married John Bentley.
Lydia, married William Boston 25 Jan 1800 in Madison County, KY.
Jamima, married Joseph Peyton, died 1811-1818.
Rebecca, born in 1788, married William F. Lock 6 Aug 1809, died after 1870 in Owen Co., KY
Madison County, KY Circuit Court Case – Edward Nelson Heirs vs. James Estill Heirs in 1811 and Bourbon County, KY Circuit Court Case – Edward Nelson Heirs vs. Green Clay in 1818.

Mrs. Edward Nelson signed depositions in 1811 and 1818 as Margaret, but some descendants of this family have passed down the name of Harriet Morgan as Edward's wife. French Tipton also gives her name as Harriet Morgan.
Nelson data from the editor's research and from that of researcher and descendant, Jackie Couture.

## MRS. GEORGE PARK

She chewed parch corn for children during siege. Says used to stand on entrails of deer &c to warm feet.
French Tipton Papers I: 81 [article on the Collins family].
[The compiler has been unable to find any information on the wife or marriage of George Park in Madison County, Kentucky records.]

## PHELPS

The Phelps family came to Boonesborough about 1778. Thomas Phelps and his family then moved to the present site of Louisville, Kentucky. His was the first double log house built there. His daughter Lucy Phelps was married to Marsham Brashear in the first wedding celebrated in Louisville. Thomas Phelps had owned land in Virginia before immigrating to Kentucky: 1570 acres in Buckingham, Lunenburg, and Albemarle Counties.

The following letter is handwritten on 2 ½ pages of legal-size paper and signed by Sarah[?] Williams DeJarnatt, granddaughter of George Phelps, Feb. 15. 1907. The body of this narrative appears to be in a different handwriting than the signature. From Phelps Family File, Special Collections and Archives, Eastern Kentucky University

My grand-father's sister, Mrs. Lucy Phelps Brashear, was a woman of short stature, rather stout, with blue eyes, and hair that had originally been brown, though it had become quite gray when I first remember her.  Her face was round and while not beautiful, she was quite good-looking.  My earliest remembrance of her was when I was about twelve years of age, when, as a widow, she came from Bullitt County, Ky. to live with her brother, Josiah Phelps, whose third wife had died.  I stayed at the home of Josiah Phelps and attended school in the neighborhood.  The house is still standing on the old county road about two and a half miles North of Richmond and still owned by one of Josiah Phelps' descendants, Thomas D. Chenaut [Chenault] Jr.

Josiah Phelps had four wives, the first _____ Patterson, who was the mother of son Jared and daughter Jane Phelps Tribble.  The second wife was Susannah Simmons, the mother of his other children.  Polly Barr was his third wife and his fourth was Martha Cameron-Allen-Massey, who survived him several years.

He entered a large body of land in the section of country around his home, and died a wealthy man at a ripe old age.

[2nd page]
In my early girlhood and womanhood I have frequently heard my Aunt Lucy Phelps Brashear speak of her exciting experience while imprisoned in Boonesborough fort, and have often heard her account of the thrilling incident of the capture of the Misses Calloway, who were also inmates of the fort, by the Indians, which has been recorded in history.

She has spoken too of her molding bullits when the men were making a defence of the fort, and that after the women went to the spring for water, while the men kept guard within the Fort, realizing that even in the savage breast there suffered[?] sufficient gallantry to prevent them from firing upon a woman.  Her life was heroic at Boonesborough and it was no less so in her ministrations to the sick in after life, especially was this true with regard to her own relatives.

My grand-father, George Phelps, whom I never saw, but of whom I have heard often, from my mother and other members of the family, was a small man, while his brother, Josiah, was of medium height & quite stout.  It is the belief and sentiment of the family that Thomas Phelps (the pioneer to Ky.) and his children George, Josiah,

[3rd page]
Lucy and perhaps others were all in the Boonesborough Fort.  As additional evidence (were it needed) of this probable —dition[?], I was present at the great Boonesborough Celebration in May 1840, and among those who sat upon the speaker's stand, were my Aunt Lucy Phelps Brashear and my grand-mother Tabitha Cummins Phelps - the sister and wife of George Phelps.

Feb. 15. 1907          Mrs. Sarah Williams DeJarnatt
Granddaughter of George Phelps

A Militia list of Bedford County, Virginia for September, 1758 names the following persons *(Henings Statutes*, VII:204):

John Phelps, Captain, Richard Callaway, Lieutenant, James Callaway [probably brother of Richard], John Martin, William Twiddy.

## LUCY PHELPS (BRASHEAR) OBITUARY

Lucy Brashear...was in the fort at the siege of the Indians at Boonesborough. She was also the first woman married at Louisville, Kentucky. Born in Campbell County, Virginia, July, 1762, the daughter of Thomas Phelps, died June 18th, 1854, at the residence of Bird Deatherage, Madison County, Kentucky. She was a sprightly acting woman until a few days previous to her death.
DM 24C 123.

## POMPEY

For a discussion of who killed Pompey, see "Pompey: The Black Shawnee", Ted Franklin Belue in *Filson Club History Quarterly* 67:5-22.]

## MATTHIAS PROCK/BROCK

Matthias Prock stated in a deposition in Davidson County, Tennessee that in 1779 he, with Squire Boone and George Phelps, drove cattle from Boone's Station to Logan's Station. *Fayette County, Kentucky Records* (Cook), Vol. I, p. 76.

Mathis Prock appears on Davidson County, Tennessee Tax Lists for 1805 and 1811. Pollyanna Creekmore, *Early Tennessee Tax Lists*, Southern Historical Press, Easley, SC, 1980.

## PROCTOR

Nicholas Proctor - born 1724 Surry Co., VA, died ca. 1790 KY. Married Nannie Smith about 1754 - she may not have been the mother of all of the 9 or 10 children. He and his five eldest sons came to Boonesborough with Capt. John Holder's Company in March, 1778.

Reuben Proctor - born 1754 Brunswick Co., VA, died Mississippi(?). Married Katurah -----. Only 3 children lived past 1824.

Joseph Proctor - born 1744 Brunswick Co., VA, died Dec. 1844 Estill Co., KY, married Polly Horn, 1777, daughter of Aaron Horn and Elizabeth Horn.

Little Page Proctor, born 1760 Granville Co., NC, died 1852 Hamilton Co., Illinois(?). Married (1) Sarah Bates. Children: Mary Polly b. 1787 Madison Co, KY. Married (2)? Sarah Jane Woodruff. Children: Reuben - b. 1796, Joseph - b. 1800 Madison Co., KY. Moved to Missouri in 1801, and Hamilton Co., IL in 1812-1814. One of the first County Commissioners there.

Benjamin Proctor - born after 1760. Married Susannah Shirley. Children: Nancy born 26 Feb 1794 Madison Co., KY. Other children: 11 children in all, mother unknown. Was a scout and Indian Spy at Boonesborough during the Revolution. Moved from Madison Co., KY 1808 to Missouri.

John Proctor - born c. 1768. Married (1) Elizabeth Hubbard 1791, Madison Co., KY. Married (2) Mrs. Sarah Green, Madison Co., KY. 12 children.

Elizabeth Proctor - born ca. 1768. Married Thomas Bennett, 1787 Madison Co., KY. 6 Children.

William Proctor - born c. 1773. Lived in KY with his brothers, moved to Missouri with some of his brothers.

James Proctor - [no dates] Lived at Estill's Station.

Mary Ann Proctor - born 1777 KY, died 1860-1870 Estill CO KY, married Thomas Noland 2 Feb 1795.

## JOSEPH PROCTOR

Estill County, Kentucky, July 1833, before Richard French, Circuit Judge of Estill County [and Keziah Callaway's son]: Joseph Proctor, resident of Estill County, aged 76 years [in a deposition given in 1839, he gave his age as 84] stated that in 1777 he lived on Holston River in Virginia. He was drafted into the militia then and served under Capt. Aaron Lewis and Col. Will Campbell on a Cherokee expedition. In 1778 he enlisted in the Virginia State Troops under Capt. Riddle and came to Kentucky, was stationed at Boonesboro, reaching that place in April 1778. He was a soldier and scout at Boonesborough and was at the "Great Siege of 1778."

In 1779 he went out under Captain [Benjamin] Logan, General George Rogers Clark commanded. He went to old Chillicothe and to Piqua Town. In 1780 he was in a campaign against the Indians in Ohio under Captain Vincent, General Clark commanded. In 1780 he was a soldier and Indian spy for Capt. James Estill. In 1786 he was in Logan's Campaign against the Indians. From 1778 he was a soldier and Indian spy throughout the Revolutionary War...

Abstracted from Joseph Proctor's Pension Statement in *Estill County, Kentucky Pensions* (Annie Walker Burns Bell): 36-7.

Joseph Proctor was a man of uncommon strength and action and is said by his compatriots to have fought with matchless daring throughout the whole engagement [Battle of Little Mountain, also called Estill's Defeat, March 1782]. At the close, the last Indian advanced upon him with a tomahawk - he raised the but[t] of his gun - the indian turned and walked off but he was so exhausted he was unable to pursue him... Irving was still alive and what was to be done with him. Proctor said he would carry him. He accordingly buckled a leather sursingle around him strapping? across his breast and under his thighs on which Irving set while he was carried in this sling by Proctor 40 miles...

Irving recovered, was very wealthy. Proctor was a Methodist preacher and as long as Irving lived he was supplied by him with a good horse &c & thus was enabled to devote his time to the preaching of the gospel about 60 years...[He] died at the age of 98 or 99.

Letter of Robert Hancock to Draper in 1853, DM 24C 22(6).

Joseph Proctor was an early Methodist preacher who was converted by preaching of Rev. James Haw at Fort Estill in 1786. He was ordained by Francis Asbury in 1809.

Joseph Proctor had a pair of scissors during the Siege of Boonesborough, the kind used for cutting up shirts, etc., which was used for wadding for their rifles. These scissors were passed through the family.

Proctor family information is abstracted from the Kathleen Noland Calder Papers, and French Tipton Papers.

## NICHOLAS PROCTOR

Deposition of Nicholas Proctor in the Town of Richmond, Madison County on the 14th day of June 1816...in a suit in Chancery in Madison Circuit Court wherein George M. Bedinger is Complainant and Wm. Martin and the heirs of Joel Walker[?] are defendants...

Question by defendant: when did you first come to Kentucky?
Answer: In the Spring of 1778.
Question: Where did you live after you first came to Kentucky?
Answer: Boonesborough.
Question: How long did you live at Boonesborough?
Answer: I lived at Boonesborough until some time in the year 1780... The people in Boonesborough lived in friendship and harmony and what one had they nearly all had, and what one knew, they mainly all knew and in a word they were as a large family.

The Bedinger Papers, DM 1A 187.

Deposition of Nicholas Proctor at Robert Miller's house...1808. I came to this country [Kentucky] in the Spring of 1778, arrive[d] at Boonesborough the 10$^{th}$ day of April. I lived in Boonesborough that summer, then at Stroud's [Strode's] station, McGees and sometimes Boonesborough. In the year 1781 I made my home at Estill's station and have continued in that neighborhood ever since.

Nicholas Proctor (signed)

Madison Co., KY Circuit Court Complete Record Book B: 334.

## PEMBERTON RAWLINGS - See also Richard Callaway

Rawlings - account opened June 26, 1775. Killed 1780. He was then engaged to one of Col. Callaway's daughters... [he was] one of the seven men who treated with Blackfish, Col. Callaway, Daniel Boone, Squire Boone, perhaps William Bailey Smith &c [at the Siege of Boonesborough in 1778].

Henderson's Ledger, DM 17CC 17.

## WILLIAM BAILEY SMITH

Major William Bailey Smith was born in Prince William County, Virginia, in 1738, and prior to the Revolution migrated to North Carolina. He accompanied Col. [Richard] Henderson to Watauga, and was present at the purchase of the

Kentucky country from the Cherokees, in March, 1775, and his name appears as one of the witnesses of the treaty. He appears to have gone on to Boonesborough in Col. Henderson's rear party, and that year explored the country as far as Green River.

The next year, he assisted in recovering the captive girls, and was at the time smitten by one of them; and in 1777, when Boonesborough was infested by Indians, he went to the Yadkin, and raised a company for its relief. Early in 1778, he was appointed Major of Clark's Illinois Regiment and raised some men for that corps; and early in June, after returning to Boonesborough, he headed a party to the Ohio in pursuit of Indians, and in a skirmish defeated them. The details show, that he was prominent in the big siege of Boonesborough, which was his last military service. [Editor's note: he may have served with George Rogers Clark in 1779.]

Returning to North Carolina, he was appointed a commissioner, in conjunction with Col. Henderson to extend the western boundary between North Carolina and Virginia, and was engaged in this service during the hard winter of 1779-80. Receiving from Col. John Luttrell, as a compensation for services rendered him, a tract of land on Green River, in Kentucky, about sixteen miles from Henderson, he settled on it in 1794. He never married, but raised some nephews whom he adopted, and [he] died at his residence on Green River, in October, 1818, at the age of 80 years. He was a man of intelligence and good sense, of fair character, rather fond of the bowl, and somewhat inclined to exaggerate his pioneer services. Though living a recluse for many years, he was cheerful and social.

In appearance, he was about six feet in height, of slender form, fine forehead, sandy hair and blue eyes. His old papers were unfortunately destroyed by the burning of his old mansion several years after his death.
Lyman Draper's Biographical Sketch of William Bailey Smith, DM 4B 251(1) note 1.

## JOHN SOUTH

...at the time the [Land] Commissioners were setting, James Estill called this Deponant & Col. Richd. Callaway to take notice as witness: that he, Estill, had made a bargain with Edward Nelson to clear out the said Edward Nelson's Settlement & Preemption on the halves or for half the land clear of all expence to said Nelson: the said Estill and Nelson were both together, & both sed [sic] that was their contract & some other persons were also present: This contract was made in Boonsborough they sed that they could not draw writings then because they could not git paper to write on at that time but when paper could be got writings was to be drawn.
[signed] John South Senr
Deposition of John South Sr, taken 25th January 1810 (in a suit of Nelson's Heirs vs. Estill's heirs). [Abbreviations spelled out, punctuation added.]

...Old John South after turning all his property into fine blooded cattle moved with his family from Virginia to Boonesborough Kentucky sometime before the [siege].

> His sons Sam & John were engaged in the battle... During the battle, the Indians killed all of the...cattle except one.
>
> After the battle the old man migrated to Bath County, Ky where he died at the age of 92 years - He was a hale & hearty farmer 6 feet 5 inches tall. His sons, John, Ben, & Sam, were often...elected Generals in the Kentucky Militia. Sam & Ben served in the War of 1812. John & Sam were in the Battle of Blue Licks under Col. D. Boone. John & Sam were elected for many years to the [Legislature] of Kentucky. Ben was for several years a member of the [State] Senate.

John South, letter 1836, from Lost Branch, Lincoln County, MO, DM 28C 34. A letter of J. W. South from Jackson KY in 1854 states that the South family lived in Maryland before moving to "the west," DM 28C 32. Transcriptions from 28C are by Jerry Parrish Dimitrov.

> Dec. 6, 1798. John South's Will, proved in Bath County (once a part of Bourbon and Scott Counties) on Jan. 10, 1820. John South, Sr., Bourbon County - wife Margaret South, 150 acres I live on, my pre-emption of 400 acres (in name of Wm. Kelly), sons: Samuel, Weldon, William, and Benjamin South, son John South; daughters: Polly, Elizabeth and Sarah. Sons William and Benjamin to have land in Madison County.

Bath County, KY Wills (Abstract from WB A: 246).

## JACOB STARNES

> ...sometime in the year 1781 he [Starnes]...with John South and others came down this creek being a branch of Licking...and camped here...and the next morning I saw John South renewing an old Improvement and at the same time he told me that he intended to lay a Warrant on that Improvement, and at the time the said South lived with me...

From Clark County [KY] Depositions, Kentucky State Archives, microfilm reel #259295, p. 273.

## DANIEL WILCOXSEN

> Shelby County, Kentucky: December 17th, 1832: he was born in Rowan County, North Carolina, 13th March, 1755. That in the fall of 1778 [probably 1777], in September, he volunteered in said county of Rowan as a private in Capt. John Holder's company - & marched to Boonesboro, Kentucky - & remained in said company at Boonesboro till 1st July, 1779, when he was ordered to Bryan's Station, & remained there till the fall of 1783, being 4 years in service at that place -three years of which he was a Lieutenant in Capt. Wm. Hogan's company & then in Capt. Robert Johnson's, in which latter he remained till fall of 1783, when he was discharged. That he resided in Woodford County, Kentucky from the time he left Bryant's, till 12 years since, when he moved to Shelby County, Kentucky.

Daniel Wilcoxsen [Revolutionary War] Services, DM 1 OO 41.

## *Petitions*

Petition from David Gass, DM 50J 18 [2 pages numbered 18, upper right corner torn off, day and year missing, but at end of petition, March 10, 1780 is date given by Richard Henderson.]
Envelope in which Petition was sent, DM 50J 20.

To<br>
Colo. George Rogers Clark<br>
---- ----- at the falls<br>
Petition from the<br>
Inhabitants of Kentucky

Major Smith

BoonesBorough March ----

Sir -
It is with the greatest concern that we find the Indians have again come out against us. They on Wednesday last tomahawked and scalped Colo. Calaway and Lt. Pemberment [Pemberton] Rollins and either killed or took two negros. They are still in our woods, and we fear will do more mischief before they return. In short, sir, we think that there will be no living in this Country without Carrying on an Expedition immediately against them, and to that End have unanimously come to a Resolution of falling[?] on some matters[?] for that Purpose - we think that nothing will so well answer the purpose as to Obtain The Governance of Colo. George Rogers Clark. If he can be prevailed on to take the command, and to Assist us with his guns, there is no doubt of success, and if he should be unwilling[?] or can't be prevailed on to go in person, We think of Colo. Linn as the next in place who wou'd answer the purpose. Upon the whole, Sir, we think the necessity[?] so great, that no time ought to be Lost. Therefore have come to a Resolution among ourselves to ----- as many fighting men from this place as possible and in order to Effect it have engaged to give Every able Bodied man who will turn out on this occasion fifteen[?] Bushels of Corn which we think sufficient to S----d them --- V-----------n. This County with the prospect of plunder and their anxious Desire of Revenging past injuries and preventing future ---- will, we Dont Doubt, Cause as many of our young men to turn out as can be spared or by any means ought to go. We further propose in this necessary Enterprize that Every man should find his own provision and be under the Command of Colo. George Rogers Clarke or some other gentleman to be so ---- ---- themselves Bound by that Solemnity of an oath --- ---- ---- the Commands of their superior officers and ----- --- to any punishment which may be inflicted by a Court Martial in case of Disobedience. This ---- ---- which we hope you will Divulge To ---- ----

[second page of petition]
of your Station and the other Neighbouring Stations Round you Whose concurrence we hope, at Least we expect. They --- ---- in an Expedition and as to the smaller matters relating to the Business we surely Cant differ   We beg you will Lose no time in communicating this matter on our part[.] Nothing shall be wanting with Respect to the Settlements on this side the River as Low[?] as Harrodsbgh and have no Doubt as to Raising the men. A Boat of Colo. Henderson's is setting off Tomorrow or next Day for the falls [of Ohio] by which we shall send an address to Colo. Clarke To superintend this matter and

obtain his answer as soon as possible. Mr. Henderson's Boat will be at Lee's town on Tuesday next and will be Convenient for you to send by and it will be needful that Colo Clark should Receive something Like an address from every principal Station. It is surely needless to arge [argue?] any thing on this Occasion we have all been Too Long sensible of the necessity and must[?] be Confident that the well-being of this Country Entirely Depends on this or some Similar Exertion and that a few weeks (if not Days) will or may be fated[?]. We are with Esteem Dr. Secy[?]. Most Obedt. Serv!

David Gass

P S We expect that Colo. Clarke will give us an answer speedily by which we will be informed whether he will undertake and when and where he will appoint a -------- or meeting of all the soldiers who can be raised.

March 10 1780
At a full meeting of the inhabitants of Boonsbgh collected[?] on the melancholy Occasion of the foregoing Letter it was [blank space?] unanimously agreed that the Sd Letter should be written which was accordingly Done and Capt. David Gass Directed to subscribe his name there to for and in Behalf of the Whole. Certified under my hand this 10th of March 1780.

Richard Henderson

~~~~~~~~~~

Persons in Kentucky who signed a petition stating the need for salt in November, 1777 who probably participated in the siege of 1778, DM 14S 14:

| | | |
|---|---|---|
| Daniel Boone | William Manifee | Pemberton Rawlings |
| William Hancock | Samuel Henderson | William Cradlebaugh |
| Caleb Callaway | Daniel Wilcoxon | Richard Callaway |
| John Holder | Richard Searcy | |
| William Hays | Reuben Searcy | |

~~~~~~~~~~

The following persons signed a petition at Boonesborough in October, 1779 and probably participated in the siege of 1778. Not all names on this petition are included below:

| | | | |
|---|---|---|---|
| David Gass | John South | Elizabeth Horn | Jesse Coker [Copher] |
| John South, Sr. | Jesse Conaway | Edward Nelson-twice | William Hancock |
| Stephen Hancock | Margaret Drake | Jacob Starnes | Samuel South |
| Pemberton Rawlings | Edward Nelson | Jesse Hodges | Nicholas Proctor, Jr. |
| John Holder | Reuben Searcy | Ambrose Coffee | John South, Jr. |
| Flanders Callaway | Moses Nelson | Nicholas Proctor | |
| John Callaway | William Cradlebaugh | | |

Endorsed: "Kentucky petition, Oct. 14, 1779 - referred to Propositions. Nov. 5 - to be heard. Reasonable," DM 14S 35.

Probable siege participants who signed a petition at the Falls of the Ohio for establishing a town there in 1780:
Squire Boone
Josiah Phelps
John Conaway
[Lucy Phelps Brashear's husband, Marsham Brashear, also signed; theirs was the first wedding at today's Louisville, Kentucky.]DM 14S 43.

## *Militia Men at Boonesborough 1777-1778*

During the late 1770's, several militia companies on enlistments of three to six months were sent from Virginia and North Carolina to Kentucky. One company arrived just after the siege of Boonesborough; this company stayed a short while and returned to Virginia, the men at Boonesborough deciding that it was too late in the year to mount an Indian expedition. The following is an incomplete list compiled by the editor of men who said they came to Kentucky with Capt. Charles Gwatkins/Watkins in 1777. Some of the men were discharged after eleven months and were present during the siege of Boonesborough. One member of the company said he enlisted in July of 1777, thus making the eleven months term end before the siege of Boonesborough. But several of the men on the list remained in Kentucky and were present at the siege (*) or were captured with Daniel Boone's saltmakers (**).

Captain Charles Gwatkins/Watkins's Company in 1777-1778:
Adam Brown [Claiborn Brown's pension statement, Richard Wade's deposition]
Arabia Brown**
John Brown** [Claiborn Brown's pension statement, Richard Wade's deposition]
Claiborn Brown [Pension statement. Relationship to the other Browns, if any, is unknown]
Richard Wade**
Benjamin Gaddy (Goddy)
Huriah Gilmore
Ancel Goodman** [Claiborn Brown's pension statement, Richard Wade's deposition]
Achilles Eubank
----- Eubank [Achilles and ----- were brothers of Thomas Eubank of Bedford County, VA who was about age 85 in 1833]
John Holley/Halley**
Jesse Hodges* [he enlisted in July, 1777, DM 11C 16]
John Milam - Lieutenant
John Preble
David Crews or Carns - Ensign
William Tracey
Joseph Jackson** - enlisted for 18 months in July, 1777]
George Richardson - ["enlisted in 1777 as a volunteer under Capt. Watkins for 6 months in defence of Kentucky, and was discharged 1778 by Capt. Watkins after serving eleven months." Pension statement in Cumberland County, Kentucky in 1832 when age 75, DM 11C 41.]

~~~~~~~~~~

The following is from a copy of the original payroll of Richard May. Names of persons who participated in or wrote about the siege are extracted from the list. [The microfilm copy of this list was barely legible, with many words very faint or smeared.] DM 17J 9-10.

A pay roll of Capt Rd. May's Company Stationed in Kentucky County in the command of Colo. John Bowman on the 13th day of July 1778 til the 2nd day August 177-(?)

Rd May, Capt

Samuel Craig, Lieut
Thomas South, Serg.
James Craig, Sergt. July 13 1778

Rank and file  Oct 7th 1778
George Phelps, Oct 7th 1778 paid to Josiah Phelps
John South
Jacob Starnes
John South Jn.
Josiah Phelps?
Thomas Phelps?, pd to Josiah Phelps
Anthony Phelps?, pd to Josiah Phelps
Daniel Trabue [Logan's Station resident whose journal is quoted in siege accounts.]

~~~~~~~~~~

Capt. Riddle's Company - arrived Boonesborough April, 1778.

Joseph Proctor                                   Matthias Horn
Nicholas Proctor?                                Aaron Horn

### Kentucky Military Pensioners 1818-1840

Those pertinent to the siege of Boonesborough:
William Beasley, Butler County. In 1840 age 78.
Arabia Brown, Garrard County, Private. In 1833 age 78, born Virginia.
Isaac Crabtree, Wayne County. In 1840 age 82.
William Cradlebaugh, Madison County, Private. In 1833 age 90, born North Carolina.
Susan Horn, Estill County. In 1840 age 77.
William Patton, Bourbon County, Private. In 1832, age 75, born North Carolina.
Josiah Phelps, Madison County, Private. In 1833, age 79, born Virginia.
George Proctor, Rockcastle County, Private. In 1833, age 92, born Virginia.
George Proctor, Fayette County. In 1834, age 74, born Virginia.
Joseph Proctor, Estill County, Private. In 1832, age 78, born Virginia.
Richard Searcy, Anderson County, Private. In 1833, age 75, born Virginia.

### Draper's List of Sources on the Siege of Boonesborough

DM 4B 252(2) [The following is a direct quote. Asterisks indicate manuscripts contained in part or full in this work.]

This detailed account of the big siege of Boonesborough, as it had long been designated by the pioneers of Kentucky, has been drawn up from the following sources:
Ms. Fleming Papers
*Ms. letter of Col. John Bowman in the Clark Papers
*Ms. Statements of Daniel Bryan
*Capt. John Carr
*Mrs. Lucy Brashear

*Robert Hancock
Maj. John L. Martin
Wyatt H. Ingram
Ms. notes of conversations with:
*Gen. Simon Kenton by Hon. John H. James, furnished by the latter to Mann Butler, the historian of Kentucky, and by Mr. Butler for this work.
*Trabue's Ms. Narrative
Virginia Ms. Archives
*Ms. notes of Conversations with Col. Nathan Boone and lady
*Moses and *Isaiah Boone
*Capt. John Gass
*Joseph Jackson
*Maj. George M. Bedinger
*Capt. Henry Wilson
*Capt. Benjamin Briggs
*W. M. Kenton

Of these, Capt. Gass, Moses and Isaiah Boone, Mrs. Brashear, and Robert Hancock, were in the fort during the siege, and the others enjoyed fine opportunities of learning the facts they furnished. The principal printed authorities consulted are, Boone's Narrative; an account of the siege dictated by *Maj. Wm. B. Smith, and published in Hunt's *Western Review*, for January, 1821; *Bradford's *Notes on Kentucky*, Marshall's *[The History of] Kentucky*, *McClung's *Sketches [of Western Adventure]*, McDonald's *[Biographical Sketches of...General Simon] Kenton*, Dr. Peck's *Memoir of Boone*, and Perkins' *Pioneers of Kentucky*.

DM 4D 184 is the Lyman Draper and Consul Willshire Butterfield draft for a jointly prepared book entitled *Border Forays and Adventures*. This book was intended for a popular audience, but Draper was unable to find a publisher. Draper says:

The following authorities here have been consulted in preparation of this Chapter: Ms. Fleming Papers. Ms. letter of John Bowman to G. R. Clark Oct 14, 1778. Ms. narrative of Daniel Trabue, a commissary at the time at Logan's Fort. Virginia Ms. Archives. Ms. Statements of Daniel Bryan, John Carr, Mrs. Lucy Brashear, Robert Hancock, John L. Martin, Samuel Millard, and Wyatt H. Ingram. Ms. notes of conversations of John H. James with Simon Kenton. Ms. notes of conversations with Nathan Boone and lady, Moses Boone, Isaiah Boone, Enoch M. Boone, John Gass, Joseph Jackson, George M. Bedinger, Henry Wilson, Benjamin Briggs, and William M. Kenton. Of these, John Gass, Mrs. Brashear, Moses and Isaiah Boone, were in the fort during the siege; as was Robert Hancock also, but too young to observe the occurrences. Boone's Narrative appended to Filson's *[Discovery, Settlement, and Present State of] Kentucky*. Bradford's *Notes on Kentucky*. An account of the siege dictated by William Bailey Smith, one of the actors, and published in Hunt's *Western Review*, for January 1821. Marshall's *[History of] Kentucky*. McClung's *[Sketches of] Western Adventure*. McDonald's *[Biographical] Sketch of[...General Simon] Kenton*. Peck's *Life of Boone*. Perkins' *Pioneers of Kentucky*, in N. A. Review, for January, 1846.

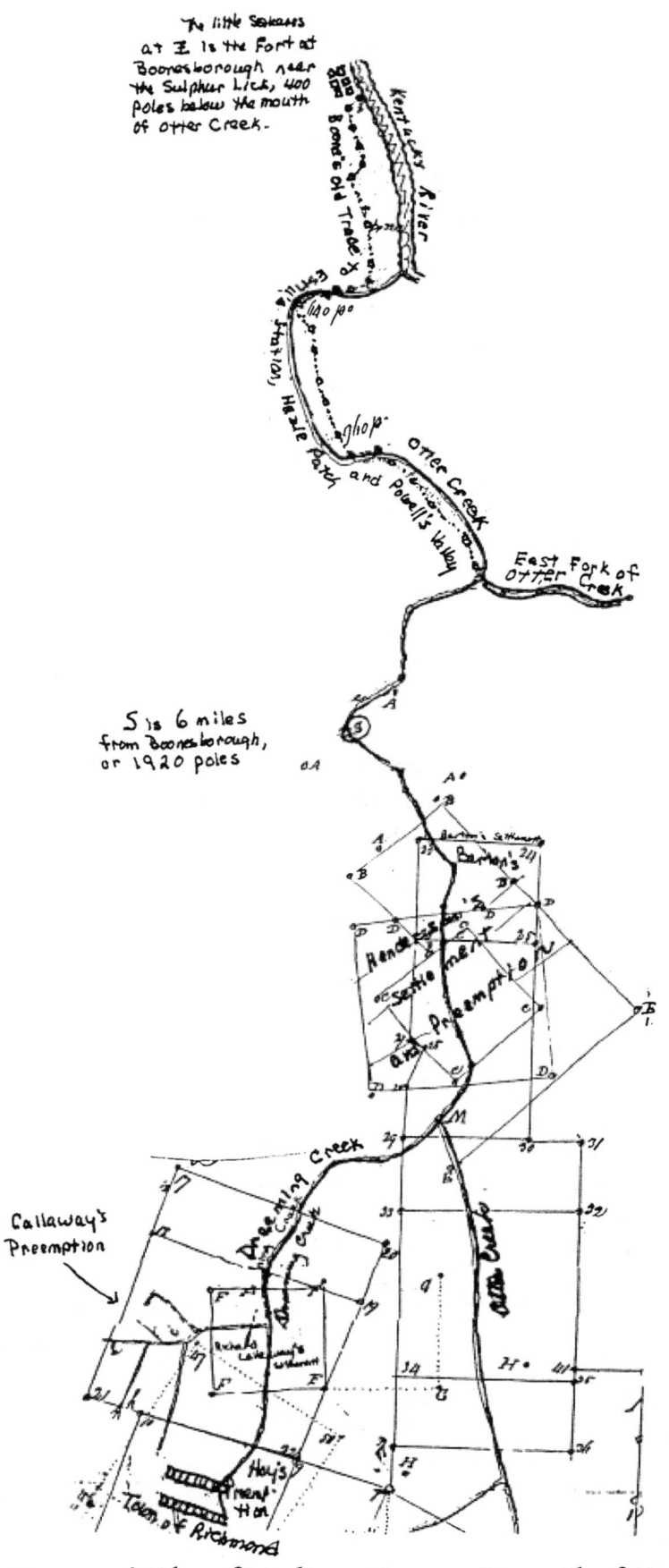

Surveyor's Plat of Madison County, Kentucky from Madison County, KY Circuit Court Complete Records Book D.

# Index

Adams, George, 49
Alexander
    Betsy, 87
    James, 87
    John, 87
Allen, Chilton, xix, 53
Anderson, Charles, 71
Asbury, Francis, 97
Baber, Harriet M., 74
Baby, Jacques, 62, 70
Ballard, Bland, 3, 53, 57
Banta, 91
Barr, Polly, 96
Bates, Sarah, 96
Beasley, William, 59, 62, 69, 104
Bedinger
    George M., 57, 83, 97, 105, 106
    Michael, 4, 51, 57
Bennett, Thomas, 96
Bentley, John, 94
Bird, Captain, 82
Black
    James, Sr., 86
    Jane, 86
Black Bird, 70
Black Fish, xviii, 1, 2, 7, 11-13, 15-19, 22-25, 50, 62, 70, 71, 83, 98
Black Hoof, 62, 70, 71
blockhouse, 3, 4
Blue Licks, 1, 9, 49, 77
    battle of, 51, 78, 89, 93, 99
    Lower, xvii, 8-10, 65, 76
Boone, 103
    Daniel, xv, xvii-xx, 1-3, 5, 7, 9-13, 15-29, 33, 35, 40-43, 47-50, 53, 54, 57, 59, 60, 62, 65, 66, 68, 71-77, 81, 83, 87-89, 98, 99, 102, 103
    Enoch, 28, 32, 53, 59, 62, 66, 76, 77, 106
    George, 59, 64, 66
    Isaiah, xxiii, 11, 17, 21, 28, 32, 36, 39, 53, 55, 59, 65, 66, 76, 105, 106
    Israel, 59, 62
    Jacob, 72
    James, 53
    Jane VanCleve, 28, 59, 62, 66, 76, 77
    Jemima: See Callaway, Jemima Boone
    John C., 1, 53, 56
    Jonathan, 59, 66, 76
    Moses, xxiii, 3, 11, 12, 16, 19, 20, 23-25, 27-29, 31, 33, 39, 41, 43, 45, 53, 57, 59, 64, 66, 72, 76, 81, 105, 106
    Nathan, xxiii, 19, 32, 35, 40-42, 45, 53, 54, 63, 71, 74-76, 105, 106
    Olive VanBibber, 2, 6, 23, 25, 34, 53
    Rebecca Bryan, xviii, xxiii, 63, 65, 73, 74, 76
    Samuel, 81
    Sarah, 59, 66, 76
    Squire, xxiii, 2-4, 19, 21-25, 27, 28, 31, 32, 34, 36, 39, 50, 53, 57, 59, 62, 66, 76, 77, 88, 89, 96, 98, 103
Boone's Station, xviii, 92, 96
Boston
    siege of, 51
    William, 94
Bouchelle, Thomas, 57
Bowman
    John, xvii, 49, 50, 53, 71, 81-83, 86, 104, 105
    Mr., 69, 88
Bowman's Campaign, xviii, 82, 90
Bradley, Edward, 22, 23, 27, 28, 59, 64, 69
Brandenburgh, John H., 63, 88
Brashear
    Lucy, 94, 103, 105, 106
    Marsham, 94, 103
Brian, John, 59, 66
Briant, David, 75
Briggs, Benjamin, 47, 53, 105, 106
Brooks
    Polly, 87, 88
    Samuel, 65
    Thomas, 88
    William, 65
Brown
    Adam, 78, 103
    Arabia, 59, 62, 65, 66, 77, 78, 103, 104
    Claiborn, 59, 62, 69, 78, 103
    Elizabeth Dooley, 59, 62, 66, 77
    Harmon, 78
    Jemima, 57
    John, 65, 78, 103
Bryan
    Abner, 79
    Daniel, xxiii, 11, 12, 15, 19, 22-25, 27, 32, 35, 36, 39, 40, 43, 49, 53-55, 59, 60, 62, 64, 72, 76, 91, 105, 106
    George, 18, 29, 48, 54, 55, 65
    Jonathan, 79
    William, 49
Bryant, Miss, 59, 62, 66
Bryan's Station, 51, 78, 100
Buchanan
    Captain, 50
    William, 54, 59, 69, 78, 81, 82
Bullock
    John, 59, 69
    Nathaniel, 65
Bundun
    David, 34, 59, 66, 69
    David, Mrs., 59
Burgoyne, xvii
Bush, William, 59, 62, 65, 88
Bush's Settlement, 83
Butler
    Mann, 105
    Simon, 9, 74
Byrd, Col., 89
Callaway
    Betsy, xvii, 18, 59, 88, 89, 91
    Caleb, 59, 67, 102
    Edmund, 59, 62, 67
    Elizabeth, 37, 62
    Fanny, xvii, 18, 51, 59, 63, 67, 88, 91
    Flanders, xvii, xxiii, 18, 29, 33, 56, 59, 60, 67, 73, 78-80, 88, 102
    Jack, 59, 78, 80, 81
    James, 59, 62, 65, 94
    Jemima Boone, xvii, xxiii, 2, 15, 18, 20, 27, 29, 37, 40, 45, 54, 56, 59, 60, 66, 67, 73, 75, 79, 88
    John, 9, 60, 67, 81, 102
    Keziah, 38, 42, 55, 59, 64, 67, 85, 91, 97
    Lydia, 59, 67, 89
    Micajah, 65
    Nathan, 37
    Richard, xvii, xviii, 12, 16, 18, 20, 23, 26, 31, 39, 48-51, 54-56, 59, 62, 67, 68, 79-81, 83, 87, 89, 91, 94, 98, 99, 101, 102
    Richard, Mrs., 59, 67
    Susan, 18
Campbell
    Arthur, 3, 5, 6, 54
    Will, 97
cannon, xx, 5, 16, 39, 48, 53
Carns, David, 90, 103
Carr, John, 105, 106
Chene, Isadore, 62, 70, 84

Cherokee Expedition, 89, 97
Chillicothe, 1, 8, 12, 13, 71, 83, 97
Clark
   G., 8
   George Rogers, xvii, xviii, 3, 24, 25, 49, 52, 53, 64, 65, 67, 80, 83, 90, 92, 97, 98, 101, 102, 105
   John, 7
   Thomas D., 54
Clay
   Cassius M., 73
   Green, 65, 73, 74, 91, 93, 94
   Samuel, 87
Clendenin, Charles, 54
Cofer/Copher, Jesse, 60, 62, 65, 88, 102
Coffee, Ambrose, 29, 60, 69, 81, 102
Collins
   Josiah, xviii, xxiii, 3, 4, 7, 13, 17, 29, 54, 57, 64, 68, 72
   William, 40, 60, 64, 69
Colyer, 84
Conway
   Jesse, 60, 62, 69, 81, 102
   John, 60, 62, 69, 82, 103
Cooper
   Sarshal, 54, 63
   Stephen, 34, 54, 57, 63, 64
Coperas Lick, 92
Cornstalk, Chief, xvii, xix, 41, 54, 93
Coshow, Evisa L., xxiii, 18, 20, 24, 33, 37, 40, 45, 54, 73, 80
Cox, Reuben, 84
Crabtree, 60, 64
   Isaac, 104
Cradlebaugh
   Didamah, 84
   Elizabeth, 84
   Susan, 84
   Sybel, 84
   William, 40, 54, 60, 69, 82-84, 102, 104
Craig
   Delinda Boone, xxiii, 12, 23, 31, 54, 75, 76, 79
   James, 104
   Mr., 75
   Samuel, 104
Craycraft, Mrs., 63
Crews
   David, 90, 103
   Dulcenia, 94

Daniel, Jesse, 21, 47, 54
Deatherage, Bird, 94
Dejarnatt, Sarah Williams, 94-96
Denny, Ebenezer, 25, 41, 55
DeQuindre, 11
   Antoine Dagneaux, 70
Detroit, 5, 6, 10, 15, 17, 49-51, 82, 85
Dillard,
   Captain, xviii
   Thomas, 3, 4, 44
Dixon
   Mrs., 37, 55
   Samuel H., 55
Doblin, Reuben, 60, 69
Donelson, Captain, xviii
Dooley, Elizabeth, 77
Drake
   Ephraim, 7, 8, 57, 60, 69, 81
   Joseph, 57, 63, 81
   Margaret, 60, 63, 67, 102
   Rhoda, 63
Draper, Lyman Copeland, xv, 55
Drouillard/Drewyer
   Frances H., 85
   George, 85
   Pelage, Mrs., 85
   Pierre, 55, 70, 85
   Sarshal, 42
Dublin, 81
Dumford, Daniel, 68
Dunkin, Captain, xvii
Dunn, Jack, 65
Duquesne, 70
   Captain, 11
Emery, Captain Will, 4, 54
Eskippakithiki, 71
Estill
   James, 64, 87, 92-94, 97, 99
   Sam, 87
   William, 93
Estill's Defeat, 51, 64, 83, 97
Estill's Station, 64, 83, 84, 86, 87, 96, 98
Eubank
   Achilles, 103
   Thomas, 103
Falls of the Ohio, xviii, 76, 80, 101, 103
False Face, 32
Fear, Edmond, 9
Finley, John, 76
flagstaff, 39
Fleming, William, 54
Floyd, John, 87, 88
Foote, Thomas, 65

French
   Richard, 48, 55, 64, 97
   Richard, Mrs., 12, 32, 42
Gass
   David, xxiii, 7, 11, 16, 23, 55, 57, 60, 64, 67, 80, 86-88, 93, 101, 102, 105
   James, 86, 87
   Jane, 87
   Jennie, 60, 67, 87
   John, xv, xxiii, 3, 11, 12, 15-18, 20, 21, 23-27, 31-35, 41-43, 45, 55-57, 60, 63-65, 67, 78, 86-88, 93, 105, 106
   Margaret, 60, 67
   Mary, 60, 67, 86
   Mitchell, 87, 88
   Sarah, 55, 60, 67, 86
   William, 60, 67, 86
Gentry
   Elizabeth, 60, 63, 69, 88
   Miss, 62
Germain, George, xvii
Germantown, 51
Gilmore, Huriah, 103
Girty, Simon, 6, 11, 88
Goddy, Benjamin, 103
Gooch, Miss, 84
Goodman, Ancel, 65, 78, 103
Green, Sarah, 95
Green River, 97, 98
Grenadier Squaw, 41
Gristham, Ambrose, 17, 56
Haldimand, Frederick, xviii, 10
Hall
   James, 57
   Susanna, 68
Hamilton, Henry, xviii, 6, 10, 11, 15-17, 19, 47, 56
Hancock
   Cynthia, 60, 63, 67
   Judith, 64, 69
   Kitty, 67
   Molly, 37, 38, 60, 63, 67
   Morris, 60, 67
   Robert, 60, 63, 65, 67, 81, 97, 105, 106
   Ruth, 38, 54, 60, 63, 67
   Stephen, 8, 54, 56, 60, 63, 67, 68, 88, 102
   William, xviii, 1, 4-6, 8, 37, 38, 41, 48, 54, 56, 57, 60, 67, 88, 89, 102
Handley
   George, 60, 63, 69
   John, 60, 63, 69

Harmon, Sarah, 78
Harris
  Hawkins, 84
  Tyree, 84
Harrison, Ben, 81
Harrod
  James, xvii
  William, 71
Harrodsburg, xix, xx, 2, 3, 50, 67, 77
Hart
  John, 60, 62, 85, 89
  Mary Irvine, 89
  Nathaniel, 79, 80, 89
  Thomas, 89
Haw, James, 98
Hays, 49
  James, 60, 63, 66
  Susannah, 63, 65
  William, xviii, 33, 34, 60, 63, 65, 66, 103
Hempstead, Stephen, 74
Henderson
  Betsy, 60, 63, 68
  Fanny, 60, 63, 68
  Nathaniel, 50, 56
  Richard, xvii-xix, 3, 22, 35, 41, 57, 68, 87, 90, 99, 100, 102, 103
  Samuel, xvii, 60, 63, 68, 87, 89-91, 103
Hendricks, George, 65
Henry, Patrick, xvii, 86
Hill, John, 60, 69
Hodges, Jesse, 8, 9, 56, 60, 64, 69, 90, 91, 103, 104
Hogan, William, 101
Holder
  John, xvii, 9, 10, 16, 33, 35, 51, 56, 60, 63, 69, 78, 79, 83, 90, 91, 97, 101, 103
  Richard P., 33, 51, 53, 56, 79, 91
  W. D., 37, 56
Holder's Defeat, 77, 78
Holley/Halley, John, 65, 104
Holston River, 92, 98
Holt, Parson, 78
Horn
  Aaron, 63, 105
  Aaron, Jr., 60, 63, 68, 69, 92, 93
  Aaron, Sr., 60, 68, 69, 92, 97
  Christopher, 63, 92
  Elizabeth, 60, 63, 68, 92, 97, 103
  Joseph, 60, 68

  Mathias, 60, 63, 68, 69, 92, 93, 105
  Nancy, 61, 68
  Peggy, 68
  Polly, 61, 68, 97
  Susan, 93, 105
  Susanna, 68, 92
  William, 61, 63, 68, 69, 92, 93
Houston, Peter, 79
Howell
  Lewis, 56
  Serena, xxiii, 29, 33, 56
  Susan, xxiii, 12, 18, 25, 27, 29, 54, 56, 79
Hoy
  Elizabeth Jones, 59, 67
  Jones, 78, 80, 81
Hundley, Anthony, 92
Ingram, Wyatt H., 106, 107
Irvine, Christopher, 89
Irving, 98
Jackson, Joseph, 65, 104, 106, 107
James, John, 28, 42, 49, 56, 74, 106, 107
Johnson
  Andrew, 7
  Andy, 49
  Cave, 72
  Robert, 101
Kaskaskia, xviii, 3, 64, 65
Keadley, Edward, 61, 63, 69
Kelley/Kelly
  Beal, 61, 63, 69
  Benjamin, 65
  William, 101
Kennedy
  John, 9
  Thomas, 83
Kenton
  Francis, 85
  John, 74
  Joseph, 85
  Simon, 8-10, 28, 32, 42, 44, 45, 49, 56, 65, 74, 85, 88, 106, 107
  William M., 106, 107
Kentucky Packet, 5, 6
Ketcham, Jonathan, 65
Kin-ni-ke-nick, 23, 57
King, John, 61, 69
King George, 13
Labade, Angeline, 85
Larouge, Rosalie Chabert, 84
Lemme, Fanny, 56

Lewis,
  Aaron, 97
  Thomas, 54
Licking River, 51, 81, 82
Linn, Col., 101
Lock, William F., 94
Lockhart, Patrick, 2, 58
Logan
  Benjamin, xvii, 49, 82, 83, 92, 97
  John, 9
Logan's Campaign, 68, 82, 83, 97
Logan's Fort, xvii-xx, 4, 7, 8, 32, 44, 45, 48, 59, 64, 65, 96, 106
Louisville, xviii, 51
Luster, Barbary, 78
Luttrell, John, 99
Mad River, 83
Manifee/Menifee
  Jarrett, 69
  William, 61, 69, 102
Mankins, James, 65
Martin
  David G., 84
  John, 7, 8, 23, 61, 65, 94
  John L., 105, 106
  William, 57, 97
Martin's Station, 51
Massey, Martha Cameron, 96
Mawmee river, 5
May
  Isaac, 84
  Richard, 64, 104
Maysville, 7
McCormack, Joseph, 49, 57
McDaniel, Robert, 82
McGary, Hugh, 93
McGee's Station, 98
McGuire, Mrs., 37
McIntosh, General, 50
McLain, Ephraim, 37, 57, 72
McMillen, John, 88
Milam, John, 90, 103
Milford, 86
Millard, Samuel, 39, 57, 106
Miller
  Henry, 72
  Robert, 98
  William, 61, 69
Mitchell, John, 86
Mockison Gap, 6
Moluntha, 17, 62, 70, 93
Monk, 87
Montgomery, Alexander, 8-10, 32, 44, 45
Moore
  Nathan, 83

Sybel, 83
Morgan, Harriet, 68, 94
Morrison, Israel, 72
Morton, John, 65
Mu----, William, 50
Navarre, Peter, 84
Nelson
    Dicy, 94
    Edward, 40, 54, 57, 61, 64, 68, 93, 94, 99, 102
    Elizabeth, 94
    Jamima, 94
    John, 61, 93, 94
    Lydia, 94
    Margarett, 61, 68, 93, 94
    Moses, 61, 68, 94, 102
    Rebecca, 94
    William, 40, 54, 57, 61, 64, 93, 94
Nicholson, Mrs., 72
Noland
    Anna Turley, 56
    Thomas, 96
Orchard, John, 61, 65, 69
Paint Creek, 9
Paint Creek Expedition, xviii, 3, 6-9, 11, 32, 45, 48, 53, 55, 57, 64, 65
Paint Creek Town, 9
Park, George, Mrs., 61, 62, 64, 69, 94
Patterson, ___, 96
Patton
    James, 71
    William, 32, 44, 45, 61, 65, 104
Paulee, Margaret, 80
Pawling, Captain, xvii
Peyton, Joseph, 94
Phelps, 43, 95, 96
    Anthony, 103
    George, 61, 64, 69, 95, 103
    Jane, 95
    Jared, 95
    John, 61, 64, 68, 94
    Josiah, 61, 64, 68, 95, 102, 103
    Katherine, 64
    Lucy, 61, 64, 68, 94
    Martha Cameron, 95
    Polly Barr, 95
    Sam, 61, 64, 69
    Susannah Simmons, 95
    Thomas, 61, 69, 94, 103
    William, 61, 68
Phillips, Indian, 1, 53, 56, 62, 70
pipe-tomahawk, 25
Piqua/Pickaway, 82, 83, 90, 97

Pogue, William, xvii
Point Pleasant, xvii, 76
    battle of, xix, 54
Pompey, 12, 13, 17, 20, 40, 41, 96
Preble, John, 103
Prock, Matthias, 31, 61, 69, 96
Proctor
    Benjamin, 61, 69, 96
    Elizabeth, 61, 96
    George, 102 105
    James, 61, 69, 96
    John, 61, 69, 96
    Joseph, 61, 68, 69, 92, 96 97 104 105
    Katurah, 96
    Littlepage, 61, 69, 96
    Mary, 96
    Mary Ann, 61, 96
    Nancy, 96
    Nannie, 61
    Nicholas, xv, 57, 64, 96-97, 102, 104
    Nicholas, Jr., 61, 69
    Nicholas, Sr., 61
    Polly, 61, 92
    Reuben, 61, 69, 91, 96
    William, 61, 96
quilting, 11
Randall, Nathaniel, 86
Reed Island, 81
Reid, Nathan, 89
Renfro, Margaret, 81
Richardson, George, 61, 62, 64, 103
Riddle
    Captain, 63, 64, 92, 97, 104
    Isaac, 81, 82
Rollins, Pemberton, xviii, 9, 22, 27, 61, 69, 79-81, 98, 101, 102
Roseman, Ann, 87
Ruddle's Station, 51, 82
saltmakers, 47
Saratoga, xvii
Scholl
    John, 80
    Septimus, 63
Sciota Salt lick, 2
Scioto, 8
Searcy
    Bartlett, 61, 62, 65
    Reuben, 61, 69, 102
    Richard, 61, 69, 102, 105
Shane, John D., xv
Sharp, Benjamin, 75
SHEL-TOW-EE, 12, 71
Shelby, Evan, 5
Shirley, Susannah, 96

Simmons, Susannah, 96
Slaves
    Amanuel, 87
    Angeline, 87
    Ann, 87
    Austin, 87
    Charity, 87
    Cube, 87
    Delphia, 87
    Dolly, 60, 62, 67, 85
    Esther, 87
    Harriet, 87
    Harry, 75
    Jack, 87
    Jake, 87
    Lieu, 87
    London, 35, 50, 61, 68
    Lucinda, 87
    Nancy, 87
    Phebe, 87
    Sarah, 87
    Silas, 87
    York, 87
Smith
    Daniel, 6, 8, 49
    Gen., 85
    Major, 50, 80, 101
    Nannie, 96

    William Bailey, xvii, xviii, 7, 11-13, 15-17, 23, 25, 26, 28, 47, 56, 57, 61, 69, 91, 98, 99, 105
Snoddy, John, 49
South,
    Benjamin, 69, 99, 100
    Elizabeth, 69
    J. W., 99
    John, 12, 23, 28, 58, 80, 99, 100, 102, 104
    John, Jr., 62, 64, 69, 99, 102, 104
    John, Sr., 61, 69, 99, 102
    Margaret, 69, 99
    Mrs., 33
    Polly, 69, 100
    Sam, 21
    Samuel, 62, 64, 69, 99 100, 102
    Sarah, 69, 100
    Thomas, 104
    Weldon, 69, 100
    William, 69, 100
Spears, Ann Mary, 82
St. Asaph's, xvii, 58
Stafford, William, xviii, 28, 29, 32, 33, 62, 65, 69

Stagg, William, 65
Stagner, Barney, xvii
Stapleton, John, 9
Starnes, Jacob, 16, 29, 62, 65, 69, 100, 102, 104
Starnes massacre, 63
Staten Island, 51
Stoner
    George W., 57

    Michael, 65
Stoner's Creek, 86
Strode's Station, 98
Sutton, Anna, 82
Sycamore Shoals, xvii
Tecumseh, 71
Thames, battle of, 81
Todd,
    Caleb, 84
    John, 2, 58
Townsend, Oswald, 62, 64
Trabue
    Daniel, xviii, xxiii, 4, 8, 20, 26, 28, 33, 39-41, 44, 47, 48, 58, 64, 65, 104-106
    James, 8
Tracey, William, 65, 103
Transylvania Company, xix, 68
treaty commissioners, 21, 47
Tribble, Jane Phelps, 96
tunnel, 40
Twitty, William, 77, 94
Twitty's Fort, xvii
VanCleve, Jane 77
Vardeman, Jeremiah, 24
Vincennes, xviii
Vincent, Captain, 97
Wade
    John, 64
    Joseph, 58, 85
    Richard, 65, 78, 103
    Richard, Mrs., 62, 64, 69
Walker, Joel, 57, 83, 97
Warens[?] Station, 83
Watauga, 90, 98
    treaty of, xvii
Watkins/Gwatkins
    Charles, xvii, 78, 90, 103
Whitley, William, 7, 56
Wilcox/Wilcoxson
    Daniel, 22, 62, 64, 69, 100, 102
    John, 76
Wilderness Road, xix, xx, 3, 48
Williams, R. G., 91
Wilson, Henry, 12, 21, 24, 58, 105, 106

Woodruff, Sarah Jane, 96
Yorktown, siege of, 51

www.ingramcontent.com/pod-product-compliance
Lightning Source LLC
Chambersburg PA
CBHW062131160426
43191CB00013B/2264